Tony Ryan
Manager
Fieldwork Services
Catholic Care
Diocese of Leeds

Previously Principal Fostering
and Adoption Officer
Department of Social Service
Leeds City Council

Rodger Walker
Resource Team Manager
Fostering and Adoption
Leeds Social Services

Previously Principal Social Worker
Department of Social Service
Leeds City Council

Story Work

Acknowledgements

We are not the first people to use life story work in our work with children, and we thank all those whose ideas we have used in developing our practice.

We thank also the children who have responded to our work and who have helped us to better understand how to communicate with them.

Through team work with colleagues and through our training days we have been able to share ideas on life story work. We have also seen, with admiration, how others have developed life story work in areas of helping which would not have occurred to us.

Our partners, Margaret and Joy, have supported us throughout our work and we would like the chance to thank them.

Finally, our thanks to BAAF for the support and encouragement we received.

Tony Ryan
Rodger Walker

Notes on contributors

Ann Atwell is a Homefinder, Dumfries and Galloway Region Social Work Department.

Rose Dagoo is a black Social Worker/Counsellor who works as a Counsellor at the Post-Adoption Centre (London) and as a Guardian *ad Litem* and Reporting Officer.

Maureen Hitcham is a Malcolm Sargent Paediatric Oncology Social Worker at the Royal Victoria Infirmary in Newcastle.

Jean Lovie is HIV/AIDS Services Development Officer, Newcastle City Council.

Gerrilyn Smith is Clinical Director of Limewood Residential Unit and formerly Principal Clinical Psychologist in the Child Sexual Abuse Team at Great Ormond Street Hospital and Course Lecturer for the Department of Health post-graduate training programme in child sexual abuse.

Contents

Introduction

ince the first publication of *Making Life Story Books* in 1985, there have been major developments in social work which have resulted in changes in practice and emphasis, particularly towards children and young people.

The Children Act 1989, as well as inquiries into child abuse, challenge in different ways all those working with children and families to re think the way they provide services, and their attitudes to those who use them. Listening to children and respecting their views and wishes is central to these developments – as it is central to life story work.

Communicating effectively with children and young people, and their families, is the only route to the type of partnership the Children Act envisages, and for those children separated from their original families it is vital if they are to understand their past and have the chance of building a solid future.

The review of adoption law also underlines the relevance of life story work. In balancing the interests of adopted people and their birth parents, openness is seen as a continuum, acknowledging that a child's feelings about contact may change over time.

Adoption is also seen as a life-long process, not as something which has an impact at only one moment in time. The increase in adoption of older children also places particular demands upon adopters in requiring them to acknowledge a child's whole past.

Life story work has its place in all these developments and this revised edition will reflect this. Life story work may not, however, be the most appropriate way to help a child, and decisions as to when and how it can help should obviously be based on experience and ideally made after consultation with colleagues.

Life story work is a way of working, not a therapeutic model. We are concerned to hear of inappropriate applications, where, for example, a child's circumstances demand skilled and long-term therapy, but life story work is used as a substitute, perhaps because resources do not permit the child's needs to be properly met.

Please don't take on life story work, or any work with children, until you understand how to do it and you have the space to do it – we owe it to children to take as much care as possible.

Why do life story work?

Children who live with their birth families have the opportunity to know about their past and to clarify past events in terms of the present. Children separated from their birth families are often denied this opportunity; they may have changed families, social workers, homes and neighbourhoods. Their past may be lost, much of it even forgotten.

When children lose track of their past, they may well find it difficult to develop emotionally and socially. If adults cannot or do not discuss this past with them, it is reasonable for children to suppose that it may be bad.

Life story work is an attempt to give back some of this past to children separated from their family of origin. Gathering together facts about that life and the significant people in it helps them begin to accept their past and go forward into the future with this knowledge. We have found that most children separated in this way gain a great deal from talking about their past, present and future to a sympathetic adult. Life story work provides a structure for talking to children. In fact everyone gains help from this process – children and adults. Interesting work has been carried out by social workers with adults (an example is mentioned in the booklist) who need to experience attention-giving and be given help in

orientating themselves. Similarly, people who are elderly get a great deal from 'reminiscence therapy', and Age Concern have produced a very helpful pack for work with groups of people, illustrating the power of nostalgia and affirming people's sense of identity.

Children separated from their birth parents, whether they are in a children's home, with foster carers, or going to a permanent new family or returning to their birth family, need to sort out why the separation occurred and why various adults have been unable to care for them. We have often failed in the past to give the children for whom we have been responsible the opportunity to do this. Our experience with the children whom we have worked with has encouraged us to believe that life story work is a useful way of fulfilling this need, and that all the children have benefited in some way.

Life story work may result in a book or video, or simply be a record of sessions which took place. It does not have to result in a product – it is the process rather than just the product which will yield most benefits for the children and young people involved.

All children are entitled to an accurate knowledge of their past and their family. This is a right that children who are secure in their families take for granted. For those children separated from their birth families, the right to this knowledge is equally important, not only for the sake of the children themselves, but also for their future children.

Life story work can usefully be adapted, not only to suit elderly people, but also the parents from whom children are separated. Many parents, whose children are currently being looked after, have been 'in care' themselves. The possibility of someone having done life story work with them is remote. However, if it is carried out with them as adults, it may help clarify the reasons, for both children and parents, for the family not being able to live together, and in so doing make best use of the separation.

The Children Act 1989 stresses that children should be involved in discussions that affect their lives. Life story work can be a means of giving the child age-appropriate information that allows them to make these informed decisions. For example, the child who discloses the identity of an adult in the birth family home who has sexually abused him or her, will need to understand that it may not be possible to return home while this situation prevails.

Life story work should complement the underlying philosophy of the Children Act 1989 – of participation and involvement of the child and his or her family. We have also heard of it being successfully used with the parents of children to help them make sense of their own past (see page 65).

What do children get from life story work?

Life story work gives children a structured and understandable way of talking about themselves. It can produce clarity where there are dangerous or idealised fantasies. Once completed, it provides them with a record which they and, with their agreement, the adults caring for them can refer to at any time, particulary when there is a crisis.

Life story work can increase a child's sense of self-worth, because, sadly, at the back of the minds of nearly all children separated from their families of origin is the thought that they are worthless and unlovable. They blame themselves for the actions of adults. If they have been abandoned, neglected or injured by their parents or wider family they are convinced that they brought it upon themselves. Life story work gives you the opportunity to show them why they should be proud of themselves, and this positive attitude should be evident in any book, video or other record which results. In talking about their birth parents, for example, although you will tell them a suitably-worded version of the truth (however

painful that may be) about their family and why they are being looked after, it is important to stress the positive side. You need to talk about their birth parents in non-judgmental terms. Perhaps you might say that not everybody is good at being a parent, but that does not mean they are bad in other respects.

When you have worked together on a book, you will feel much closer to the child. We have found that memories of our own childhoods are always awoken. If we, too, have experienced pain, we share this with the child – while always remembering whose story it is! Some people do life story work with more than one child at a time, and some sharing of experiences – without breaking confidences, of course – can make a child feel better. Thus a child can appreciate that many people experience pain in their childhood and that the fault does not lie with them; they need not feel guilt, as so many children amazingly do, for their parents' behaviour.

Finally, you need to be able to relax and enjoy at least some parts of each of the sessions and, for this, you may need to re-learn how to play. This will give you a lot of fun! With some of the play techniques suggested later on, you will need to get down on the floor with the child and play with toys. Self-consciousness is not a virtue in this situation but, if you need a reason, you should know that your playing has a serious purpose and is a valuable technique, and as important as being able to talk naturally to a child on important issues. While not all life story work will lead you into play, some will and you might as well enjoy yourself while you are playing!

About identity

A healthy sense of identity is vital to everybody. A poor sense of identity can disable children and adults alike, and limit their ability to take on fresh challenges. For some children one of the major challenges of their life will be moving into a new family. At its worst a poor sense of identity can 'freeze' children so they have an over-investment in the past and cannot move on to think about the future. It can also cause apathy and a depressed, fatalistic outlook.

Identity is a complex concept; it probably starts in individuals with the first separation of the 'inside' and 'outside' self at about six months. This creation of the idea of 'self' is crucial to healthy development and where it is hindered by events and by other people who are important (like mothers and fathers) not responding appropriately, severe problems can arise.

Whilst an understanding of the 'self' is difficult, particularly for children severed from their roots and without a clear future, it is made easier by separating out some of the more easily definable parts and discussing them openly with a child. One way of doing this is to talk about the past, the present and the future.

The past is made up of places, significant dates and times, people, changes, losses or separations and other events, both happy and sad, like illnesses, holidays and birthdays.

The present is made up of self-images, reactions to the past and responses to questions like What am I doing here? Where do I belong? How do others see me?

The future is made up of issues such as What will I be? Where will I live? What chances do I have? What other changes will there be?

Many children we have worked with have felt miserable and depressed. Looking to the future should be about easing these feelings and replacing them with hopes and aspirations. In life story work with a child, issues relating to the past, present and future can be raised in ways that feel natural to a child. This will give you and the child opportunities to establish facts about the past and present and go some way towards demystifying events and people in the child's life. Similarly, hopes and doubts about the future can be raised and 'bridging' (linking the past to the future) into the new family or situation can begin.

The section on identity theory is necessarily brief and you may want to read more authoritative views. We have listed books for further reading at the end of this book.

Who should do life story work with children?

We firmly believe in the healing effect of talking. Any sympathetic adult who is prepared to spend the time and give the commitment to the child by making a life story book, video or any lasting record to which the child can add and refer back to, can be the right person to do it.

Anyone who takes on this task will need to enlist the active support of the child's social worker and significant others through regular discussions. We have successfully helped adoptive parents and foster carers and many residential social workers to work with children in this way. It is also important – as the spirit of the Children Act encourages – to make a genuine attempt to include the birth family, although the child will always be the guide to the extent of their involvement.

What does life story work require of you?

Whoever undertakes life story work with the child needs to be alert and have patience in order to pick up any clues that the child may reveal, particulary during sessions when not a lot is happening because the child is not in the mood or is testing if you can be trusted. The person also needs to be sensitive to the child. There is no blueprint for life story work, but the child is always the key. It is your responsibility to find ways of letting the child tell you about his or her life, and avoid imposing your own views. Whilst you should not allow patently false information to be recorded, you also need to avoid taking over and producing the 'Authorised Version' of a child's life. It is the child's life story after all, and it is how he or she views it that is important.

It is also important to convey to the child that the record can be altered. Some children will disclose important information at a later date, which they will wish to add to their life story.

There are mistakes which less experienced workers sometimes make but which should, with common sense, easily be avoided.

1 Never betray the child's confidences made to you. *

2 Don't avoid talking about things the child wants to talk about because they make you uncomfortable.

3 Don't put words into the child's mouth.

4 Once you have taken on life story work, you must not abandon the child halfway through it and hope

that someone else can complete your work. You should continue with it until both of you agree it is time to end your regular sessions on it.

5 Never use either the end product or carrying out life story work as either a prize or a punishment, but only as a normal part of your life together.

6 Go at the child's pace not yours – it's actually quicker this way! Rushing children only makes them slow down or skimp on details.

7 Be consistent – the child has to know when you are coming. Don't start work and then say you'll be back when you've got time. A child will not trust you and will feel hurt if you do this.

* If a child discloses to you for the first time that he or she has been sexually abused it must be made clear to the child that some information will have to be passed on to those adults responsible for their protection (See also Chapter 13, *Working with children who have been sexually abused.*)

When might you do life story work?

Life story work can be started at any time when the adult and the child have enough confidence in each other to begin and the time to continue. Sometimes it is part of preparing a child who is going from a children's home to a family; sometimes it can help the child accept life as it is.

Ideally, the decision to do life story work will come at a review or case conference. At the same time it will be decided who does what and where. Everyone involved should then support the adult making the book, feeding them with facts and information and suggesting ways around problems. A foster carer or adoptive parent should look for support from their social worker and perhaps from other substitute parents, and have regular discussions about progress. Equally, if you are a social worker or residential social worker, good supervision is very important.

Other members of the 'team' involved with the child who hear of the child progressing or regressing should tell the adult doing the life story work about it. They should also be prepared to cope with the child reliving past experiences or looking for reassurance and possibly displaying disturbed behaviour. They need to understand that this is all part of the healing process.

Feedback to the 'team' is also useful in reaching appropriate decisions about the child's future. However, it is important to repeat the warning about not betraying the child's confidences to you.

How do you deal with confidentiality?

The question of keeping confidential what a child tells you while undertaking life story work together is an important one, to which we have given much thought. Throughout the time we have worked with children we have tried to reach a satisfactory solution to the conflict between not betraying the child's trust and yet needing to share some of the information with others.

One of the difficulties is that the significant adults in the child's life, such as foster carers, social workers and residential social workers, may have a 'team' approach. They will feel that it is important to pool knowledge with the goal of helping the child. He or she, of course, will not regard this in the same way. Whenever possible try and include significant people from the child's past.

We have always found in our individual work with children that they want your discussions to remain confidential to the two of you. Children may disclose something of their inner world which they are not prepared even to record in a life story book. For example, they may express anger against a person in their past which may have relevance for the future and you may feel it necessary to pass it on to others. In such circumstances, we would share the outline of the confidence only, without disclosing any details.

We always make it clear to the significant adults that their child will probably demand confidentiality about certain things and that we intend to respect this. It may be possible to explain to the child that you would like permission to talk to others about a particular disclosure because you believe it may help him or her. You might be able to negotiate with the child what you are allowed to say. This in itself can be helpful to the child because it provides another format to discuss a possible painful event in the past. However, disclosures are sometimes so serious that you cannot keep silent, for instance, if the child knows of a sexual abuser still actively abusing children. You can think of other instances yourself relating to issues of protection and self harm.

In such cases, you will have to explain to the child that you must share information in order to protect him or her and/or other children. What you can promise is that you will not share the information unless absolutely necessary, that you will stand by the child, be present at any interviews and assure the child he or she will be protected against the abuse. You can also, within reason, agree with the child the timing of sharing the disclosure. In general, the only thing that stops a child disclosing abuse is a belief that nobody can help or protect them. A child will disclose to you if you gain his or her trust – be careful not to betray that trust.

How does life story work end?

There comes a stage when you both agree that you have reached the present day and covered everything you can, and that the regular sessions can end. This point is different for every child. However, you should be suspicious if the life story work has turned into little more than a photograph album and you are finished after only three or four sessions. In that situation, go back over what has been produced, and see if the child can write or draw about any particular period which you know (from the file or doing a questionnaire, as described later) to be sensitive.

We never regard the work as finished but some record of the process is important as it provides a reference point, particulary as it can be updated until adulthood. It can be turned to in a crisis, such as when a child revives a ghost or a myth from the past, or is beginning to discover and remember parts of the childhood not available to them when they started on their life story work. Then you can go to the section of the book which dealt with it and gently rediscover or redefine the reality together.

We often find, for example, that when we discuss a new permanent family with a child, he or she will start to make up fantasies about their birth family, however badly they let them down. Children have a natural fear of letting go of their present relative security – however unsatisfactory that may be – to face a risky future. Life story work can be helpful in looking back together at the anger the child felt about the birth parents when originally doing the life story book. This may help him or her to let go more easily and face the future.

Welfare 'checklist'

Increasingly, courts are expecting social workers to have worked with a child to find out what the child might want to happen and why. In coming to a decision about the paramount interests of the child a court will pay attention to the welfare 'checklist', which is a list of the factors the court needs to take into account in arriving at a decision, for example, about whether to make a section 33 order.

Life story work can help a child and social worker to reach agreement on what to say to the court. We particulary point to the first four parts of the checklist mentioned below. The court must take into account:

a) the ascertainable wishes and feelings of the child concerned (considered in the light of his or her age and understanding);

b) his or her physical, emotional and educational needs;

c) the likely effect on him or her of any change in circumstances;

d) his or her age, sex, background and any characteristics which the court considers relevant.

Part b) of the checklist requires the court to hear what his or her emotional needs are, and part c) highlights the need for a child to have thought through, with a social worker, what effect change will have on him or her. Agreeing what these are should be part and parcel of life story work.

This book is the result of our own experience. We have written it to help others who want to use life story work as a way of helping children. We hope that what we have said here will help and not discourage you. You may worry that you might damage a child or give him or her too much pain. If you have a commitment to the child, you are the right person to undertake life story work and you will more than compensate in the long term for any pain the child might suffer in the short term. The only damage you can do is by walking away from your commitment before it is completed.

2

Communicating with children

These 'Ten Commandments' quoted directly from *Opening New Doors* by Kay Donley, former director of Spaulding for Children, an agency in New York, in our opinion 'say it all' when it comes to communicating with children. While the terminology reflects the American public care system, the message is universal.

1 Avoid cliches in talking to children.

Children recognise cliches and your use of them will readily and clearly inform the child that you are indeed an adult who does not know how to talk to them. Some of the typical cliches that adults use in working with children are questions, probing questions, such as, 'How do you like school? Which class are you in?' Never begin a conversation with a child in that way. Eventually, when you really know the child, such questions may be appropriate, but never as an opening gambit. The best way to begin a conversation with a child is simply to exchange some pleasantries about who you are and how pleased you are to know him and let it go for a while. Children are more responsive to the idea of approaching you gradually, than to being physically and psychically overwhelmed by this large thing that flies at them and begins to probe their innermost thoughts. Take your time. You never know at first if you have a very shy, withdrawn child or a very aggressive one.

2 Assume that any child you are going to work with has some deep concern that has never been adequately understood or answered.

I am referring specifically to children in public care, all of whom typically share the experience of having been separated from their parents. In many cases they have also lost a succession of care-takers – house parents and foster parents. In working with the child you may, in fact, discover that someone very skilled and very sensitive has helped him to understand what has happened. But it is safer to assume that no one has adequately assessed the deep and often confused concerns of the child.

3 Understand from the beginning that children in care have been hurt; some part of them has been damaged.

Never make the assumption that because everyone presents this child as untouched and undamaged, he or she must be that way. More often than not, the child will have been handled by a lot of unperceptive people. Perhaps this particular child has made an exceptionally good adjustment in the face of difficult and painful circumstances. But as a rule, there are always some damaged pieces of unfinished business tucked away. If you understand that, you will not be dismayed or thrown off balance six months later when someone says: 'You know, there's something peculiar about this kid. He's not quite what I would call 'normal'.'

4 *Remember that in working with a child your essential task is to learn how he explains himself to himself, and what he understands his situation to be.*
Unless you really know what is going on inside him, you will not be able to represent him justly or truthfully to residential staff or to potential foster or adoptive parents. It is not simply that you must know where this child is for your own satisfaction. You must be prepared to communicate your understanding to other people. This is not easy.

5 *Develop specific concrete tools which will help you communicate with children.*
Children are not normally interested solely in verbalisation as a way of communicating with anyone. They have other available tools and you must find out what they are so that you can use them too.

6 *Be prepared to become a dependable, predictable and regular fixture in the child's experience.*
You simply cannot pop in on a Monday and say, 'I'll see you again sometime soon.' The social worker's indefinite promise of returning to his life usually means avoiding him for several weeks and then popping in again. This simply does not work and is, in fact, destructive. You are adding to the child's already increasing fund of knowledge that, as far as he is concerned, adults are undependable, unpredictable and unknowable. You must regularise your contact. Most social workers say, 'I really would like to, but I haven't the time.' This begs the question, because it is possible to regularise contacts, even if there are long intervals between visits. It is the idea of predictability that is important to the child. If you make a commitment then you keep it. (And I mean you keep it, even if it breaks your back!) If, for some reason, you are unable to keep the appointment you have made, it is important that you communicate directly with the child the reasons why you cannot. I have known workers go to the extent of sending a telegram to a child whom they could not reach by telephone, so strong was their sense of commitment.

7 *Remember that each child's experience is unique and that it is absolutely crucial that each child is helped to begin to come to grips with his life.*
You cannot begin on the assumption that, because you have worked successfully with one or two children who have been neglected by their parents, you know what this experience means to any child. Certainly, you can learn from one situation and apply your knowledge to another. But keep in mind that you are dealing with individuals: deceptively similar experiences have very different meanings for different children.

8 *As you work with a child over a period of time, you must help him develop what I call a 'cover story'.**
'Cover story' is not a very good phrase because a lot of people think that I mean concealing things and I do not. I believe that a child must have a clear, understandable, acceptable explanation of his circumstances, which he must be able to use at will and comfortably. For example, when he goes to a new school, he will be meeting a lot of new children, making friends and meeting people living in the neighbourhood. He will be asked questions about himself and it is essential that he should have a socially acceptable and logical explanation for who he is and where he is and why he is in this situation. Only too frequently, unskilled workers do not appreciate how essential this is and do not help the child develop a 'cover story' for public consumption. Without it the child is left to his own devices and frequently falls into fabrication. A child fabricates when he is not quite sure how people will receive the true facts of his situation. Fabrication, once found out, will very quickly give the child a reputation in the neighbourhood for being a spinner of tall tales, or at worst, a liar.

My best friends!

* *For children who have been sexually abused it may be more helpful to think in terms of privacy of 'good' and 'bad' secrets. Such children may have a version of events in their life for public consumption, and one they share with significant and trusted adults.*

9 *Commit yourself always to what I call a multifaceted or composite view of the child.*
Remember there is no one true way of seeing and experiencing a youngster. Every person who has contact with the child will have a slightly different point of view and a unique experience. Some people will be enthusiastic about him, while others cannot abide him. What you are really searching for is a combination for all those perceptions, because buried amongst all of them there is the truth. Somewhere, amongst all those varying views of the child, will be a perception that his potential adoptive parents may make of him. So it is important that you begin to develop that kind of sensitivity and awareness.

10 *Keep in mind from the beginning of your work that you are obliged to convey to any care-takers – be they residential staff or adoptive families – a true sense of the child's history.*
You may think that this is self-evident and that I am being needlessly repetitious in stressing this point. But I think it bears repeating, because many social workers feel they are doing a child a grave injustice by telling the full and sorry tale, and that the only way to spare the child is to conceal certain things. These are usually things the social worker finds distressing or unpalatable, so they are concealed because she feels that this will give the child a better chance in life, a better opportunity for placement, an easier adjustment. Invariably those very things come flashing up anew out of the child's history and past to create problems and difficulties for him and his care-takers. This is a painful area for most social workers but it is one which you must grapple with and come to terms with.

Extract from *Opening New Doors*

Before you begin

The idea of life story work should grow naturally if you talk and listen to what children say about their family and why they think they are separated from them. There are, however, guidelines which draw on Kay Donley's work as described in her 'Ten Commandments'.

1 The aim, both initially and throughout the period of doing life story work, is to show the child that you are interested in him or her and that there is no limit to what you can be told. You can make it clear that you would like to know lots more about him or her and so will be visiting regularly and getting to know them.

Remember that you are talking to a person who happens to be a child and a client. This means that he or she is about as interested in telling you about how they are getting on at school as you would be in telling a stranger about how you are getting on at work. Every other adult will have asked them how they get on at school, and they know it is just a conversational ploy used by strangers. When you have got to know the child and he or she knows you are genuinely interested, they may tell you honestly how they feel about school.

You need not say anything of great meaning at first, but simply convey that you will be coming to talk to the child about him or herself and to perhaps make a book about their life. Each child will work at a different pace, just like adults, and you should allow the work to happen naturally; any child will let you know when they want to be friends with you.

2 Should you feel the need to approach the idea of making a life story book or video cautiously or slowly, you could start with a questionnaire book, which we describe later.

3 When the life story work is undertaken by someone not living with the child, it should always take place at set times which you faithfully keep to. Don't just say, 'I'll see you in a week or two.' Make a date and keep to it. If you cannot keep an appointment, ring up and speak to the child personally, say why you cannot come and say when you are going to come next. You will probably be the first person in the child's life to do this and it will bring forward the day when he or she learns to trust you.

4 If you are living with the child, you should be able to talk together at any time that is mutually convenient. In addition there should be regular times set aside so that the child does not have to be responsible for continuing the work. You must not just allow the topic to drift and find that weeks go by without the work progressing.

3

Before starting life story work

Initial research

You need to inform yourself about the child's 'official' background before you start to work together. If you are a social worker, you will have access to the child's file. If you are an adoptive parent or foster carer and it has been decided that you will be helping your child to do some life story work, then your child's social worker should provide the information. Don't be afraid to badger until you have all the information you need. If you meet difficulties, exercise your right to call a review to 'iron out' any problems.

Read the information about the child carefully and thoroughly. Collate the information in chronological order, noting the reasons given for decisions, the reasons for moves and so on. Make a note of any gaps in the records so that you can obtain information about these periods. From this research you will be able to construct a 'life graph' for the child. We show an example on page 30, where we discuss life graphs in detail.

It may be at this stage that a worker discovers that there are indicators which might suggest a child has been sexually abused. Workers will then need to decide what to do with this information. It can be very helpful for looked after children who have not yet disclosed their experience of sexual abuse to have an adult 'guess' that sexual abuse was something that

was going on in their family of origin. Often no-one has sat down and reviewed the whole of the child's file in this manner before. It is extremely important to ascertain whether or not a child has been sexually abused in their family of origin before contacting the significant people in the child's life. Sex offenders will often go to great lengths to silence the children, and renewed contact can act as a trigger both for traumatic memories for the child, and for renewed attempts by the adults to silence the child again.

Using the information you have gathered, write immediately to significant people in the child's life. (They may take time to respond and you want to have this information available when you need it.) Explain about the life story work, and if a book is planned ask for information and the loan of photographs and other documents. It is important to emphasise that photographs can be copied and returned to the sender, or that they can send copies.

We give overleaf an example of the kind of letter that you might send in order to get such information.

The material you ask for may well be very slow to arrive or may never arrive and you will have to depend upon other aids.

Mrs M Croft
7 New Town Estate
Westfield

Dear Mrs Croft

I have recently started visiting David to help him
prepare a book about his life before he came to live
at Eastfield Children's Home. Already I have obtained
several photographs for him to include but I have no
photographs of when he was very young, nor any of you.

Photographs, I realise, are very precious but nowadays
they can be easily copied. If you have any photographs
I would be grateful if you would loan them to me and I
would return them as soon as I had obtained copies.

I look forward to hearing from you and perhaps coming
to tell you more about David's book.

Yours sincerely

My
birth dad.

Following up the background

Whenever possible, the child's social worker should visit significant people in the child's life to gather further information to help to form as complete a picture as possible. These people may include the birth parents and wider family, children's home staff and former foster carers. Again you will need to write first to let them know the purpose of your visit.

Birth parents and their extended family

Do not be afraid to approach birth parents, even if it is a long time since they saw their child. Those involved with a child are usually anxious about this. They may say, 'She has forgotten her mother... Why stir up the past?...It will only push her mother into making trouble...' Such worries are genuine. Obviously a birth parent should not be approached if this might cause harm to the child, but be sure of your own motivation if you decide not to ask for the birth parents' help. Is it to protect the child or to protect yourself?

When we first started to approach birth parents we were worried about the damage we might cause. Perhaps we have been lucky, but we have never ceased to be amazed by birth parents' willingness to co-operate.

Usually it is only the birth family which can provide the information to make a family tree, one of the best ways of showing a child where he or she 'came from', which we discuss later.

Often, when a child's parents were not married, the birth mother will provide information about the birth father. Perhaps it will be the first time she has been asked about him in a way that seems relevant to her. She might reveal such insights for the child as 'He had blue eyes', or 'He was six foot tall', or 'He loved the countryside', or 'He was good with animals'. It is unlikely that in her contact with officials, she will ever have been asked for this kind of information.

Where the father of a child is not known, there may have been good reason for the birth mother to have concealed his identity. The number of children born as a consequence of incest is very difficult to assess, but there are certain patterns of sexual abuse within families which suggest that a child might be the product of incest. It may, of course, be an open secret and be documented on the child's file. Such information will need to be handled very sensitively

for the child. It is important, therefore, not to assume that the context in which a child was conceived was necessarily one of a loving relationship. Having a child as a result of incest can have negative consequences in terms of the birth mother's parenting abilities. This would be important to convey to the child – that the birth mother was perhaps constantly reminded of things she wished to forget whenever the child was around.

She might also provide an account of her own childhood. This can often help her child to understand and come to terms with being unable to live with her. Sometimes the child will learn that one parent has either been separated from their original family or had an unhappy childhood.

Children's home staff

Many children will have lived in several children's homes. Staff, especially cooks, cleaners and gardeners, who have worked in a home a long time, will have photographs which you can borrow. These may be of the child in a group, or of the staff or of the home itself.

Foster carers

If a child has lived in a foster family, they will often have photographs of the child and the family. They are also a source of information to draw upon in life story work.

Be prepared to exercise imagination and flair in obtaining photographs, treasures, school work, old toys – anything that helps children to understand that they have a past and gives them a sense of identity and belonging.

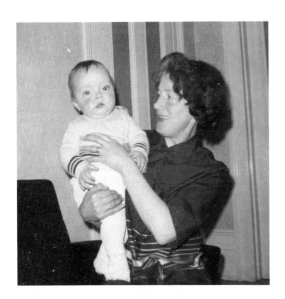

My birth Mum.

4

Getting started

There is no set procedure for life story work. The approach we take may not be suitable for you, and you will discover your own approach. Remember, too, that the goal is not necessarily to produce a book or video. You may be documenting sessions in different ways, but whatever is produced will belong to the child.

Meeting the child

Each session should focus on the task of getting to know the child in order to make progress with the life story work. This means – and we repeat this because it is so important – that you become a regular, reliable and predictable person in the child's life. Make appointments and keep them.

David, whose life story book is occasionally used to illustrate this book, obviously thought that adults were untrustworthy and unreliable. He said at our eighth meeting, 'You always come on the day you say you will, don't you?'

How long should a session last?

The length of a session will depend on a number of factors: whether the child lives with you, the child's span of concentration, the time you have available. Ideally, you should set a specific time for each session. We find that an hour is perhaps the maximum time we can hold our own concentration, and, for this

reason, we usually structure the session to last roughly that long.

If the child lives with you, perhaps the weekend is the best time for these sessions because you both may be more relaxed and free from week-day pressures.

How often will you meet?

Kay Donley in her 'Ten Commandments' states that you should become a regular and consistent person in your child's life. What is meant by 'regular'? We feel that in the early stages, say the first eight to ten weeks of working with a child, you should aim for weekly sessions. However, you may find that once a fortnight, though less satisfactory, is more realistic. Try to avoid raising your child's expectations by frequent contact in the first three or four weeks and then becoming erratic in your later contact.

Surprisingly, if you are either a residential social worker, foster carer or adoptive parent and your child lives with you, it can be difficult to arrange regular sessions. It is often a problem to find a mutually convenient time within the domestic and social rhythms of the household. A person outside the household can interrupt these rhythms more easily. A foster carer's free time can clash with a child's time, for example, when he or she either wants to watch television or play with friends.

The most important aim is that the life story work is started and the sessions on it are consistent. It may seem a large commitment and this could deter you. Vera Fahlberg, a psychotherapist with considerable experience of working with children who have experienced difficulties and their families, states that 'tomorrow is made harder by lack of preparation today'. In other words, this is time well spent and may eventually save you time by helping to ensure that your child's placement does not break down.

What materials do you need?

Apart from the photographs and other documents, all you need to produce a book is a looseleaf folder and paper, and it is useful to have pens, coloured pencils and glue handy for drawing, writing and putting pictures into the folder. A looseleaf folder allows you to make corrections and to add new material as it comes to light.

Children who are looked after often experience educational difficulties and it is important that they are not made to struggle with writing. You can help them with spelling, if requested, but avoid correcting any mistakes. Some children enjoy dictating for you to write or type; or you could write in pencil for the child to go over in ink. Always remember that this is the child's own private book, not a show piece. Be prepared for it to be somewhat untidy and messy and allow the child to include anything he or she wants.

Who else should be involved?

You need to work away from distractions and interruptions. However, it is important to have another adult involved in the work, although not part of the session. For example, if you are a foster carer, the child's social worker will have to provide most of the factual information and seek out photographs. As the work progresses, the child might wish to show and talk about the life story to this significant adult, who has helped in this way. Doing so may help you to ascertain how the child is absorbing and under-standing the past. As the project progresses, members of the birth family may also be regularly involved.

Who keeps the life story work?

Without question it belongs to the child. Should he or she, therefore, be allowed to keep it? Of course, but the timing is important. Some would argue that as the book belongs to them, the child should always keep it. This is the ideal and should certainly be what happens towards the end of the time you are working together. However, at certain stages some children destroy their life story work if it is in their possession. The child may be overwhelmed by a sense of anger and frustration about what has happened and may direct this at the book. If this happens, valuable photographs

and documents may be lost forever. (We now take photocopies of documents which cannot be replaced.) In the early stages, therefore, we recommend that you are prudent and make sure that the book is kept in a safe place. At all times the child should have reasonable access to it, but this needs to be supervised.

It may also be worth considering using a ring binder if a book is being produced, so that children can edit bits in or out. For example, a child's emotional response to a particular adult in their life may be affected by current issues that they are discussing. This is especially relevant for children who have been sexually assaulted and have not disclosed at the time of their life story work. There may be a picture of them with the perpetrator in their book. Whilst the child may at some point in the future like to reclaim positive feelings they had for their parent who sexually offended against them, it may be that at this point they are unable to experience positive feelings.

You may decide to provide a photo album separately too, and this alleviates the problem of how to keep the book safely and yet share it with your child.

Usually we find that the best time to give the book, or whatever else is produced, into a child's own keeping is when the child has joined the new family and is showing signs of being secure with them. It may well become a proud possession which the child wants to show to others. A social worker in Northern Ireland comments in *Life Books for Children in Care*, 'Through their life books, our children have come to own their own story little by little, mainly because they have gone through them so often with other people and each time it becomes clearer to them. Besides, in retelling it, they think of new questions to ask and gain new realisations each time.'

Who can look at the life story work?

The answer is no one – without the child's permission. This, of course, is another element of confidentiality. Nonetheless, encouraging the child to share the product of his or her life story work should be a feature of your work. For example, foster carers might suggest that their child talk about the book with their social worker. If the child agrees, it can provide an opportunity to talk about events in their life. An additional bonus can be that the person who is helping the child make the book can gauge the level of understanding from the way their child talks about the past. But you must be sure that the child really wants to share the book and is not just agreeing to please you.

It is implicit from the beginning of doing life story work, where the plan is to place a child in a new family, that the new family will be shown whatever is produced. This is made easier because we always include the child's anxieties and aspirations for the future in life story work. For example, the child's desire to own a bicycle or to remain in contact with someone from the past. One girl, worried about how she might be punished by her new parents, wrote in her book, 'It is alright to be smacked, but not to be hit with a belt.' Through life story work, children can have a safe way of making known their expectations to their new family, and perhaps to offer past experiences to talk about.

We have found that, as they move towards placement, many children allow their prospective family to look at their book. From the other side, we encourage the prospective families to make their own life story book for the child to see. Children appreciate this gesture and it can be a very good 'ice breaker'.

What problems will you face?

In taking on life story work, you can expect some regression from the child as a matter of course. By 'regression' we mean a return to behaviour which might have been left behind, or taking on behaviour patterns which belong to a much younger age group. A common experience, for example, is that the child's behaviour will go back to that appropriate for the age at which they were first separated from their family.

Everyone has their own way of dealing with these problems. However, regressive behaviour will not persist and we have never taken it as a sign that we should discontinue life story work. If children find life story work too threatening, they simply will not do it and will make it quite clear to you, not simply regress for a period. (We discuss regression further in the next chapter.)

How will the work affect you?

As we have said before, you should never betray the child's confidences and should not avoid talking about the things the child wants to talk about because they make you feel uncomfortable.

Most of us have also experienced feelings of loss and separation. Working with children who are unravelling their own sufferings may release some of these feelings within yourself. It is important that you have help and support from someone you can talk to about what is happening to you. If you are a foster carer, your local foster carer group may be able to help. Some of these groups hold regular meetings for foster carers who are helping their children with life story work. Other people may turn to the child's social worker for support, and social workers to their colleagues.

Be honest, but not brutal

Every child is hurt by separation from their family. Use this knowledge in talking to the child. Many of the other adults in a child's life may tell you that he or she is completely untouched by it and never wants to talk about it. You must know better, and work to allow the child to express this hurt and anger at some stage. They will want to do this, but may never have found anyone who has been trustworthy enough to tell. You may be the first person who has gained their trust in being consistent in wanting to know all about them.

Don't impose your version of events on the child, as many adults will have done. You want to find out what the child thinks about what has happened. If you disagree with what you think is fantasy, say so, but be no more authoritative than you would be in disagreeing with another adult.

It may be helpful for you tell the child what you think may have happened, particularly if there are indicators of undisclosed abuse in the family of origin. It may be that the abuse is clearly documented in the social work file, but the child appears not to remember. Acknowledging how awful life has been in their family of origin may be an important step for traumatised children to move forward in their lives and begin the process of recovery.

Be honest, but not brutal. If you cover up or prevaricate, the child will know it and will not trust you as much. If you side with children in running down their parents or others, you will find later that they will not be honest with you when talking about their past or their feelings about others. Try to identify some positive features about people they complain about, but don't cover up the negatives. Try to be even-handed and objective about why people do things and children will trust you more than if you join in a tirade against their family and friends. Remember that their birth family is part of them; criticising the family will eventually feel like criticism of them.

Finally, remember that every child is an individual with a very interesting story to tell if you can help them to do it. Let them know that you are interested and can be trusted and eventually they will want to tell you all about themselves.

Some questions answered

We have made it clear throughout that life story work with a child can be fraught with difficulties. If you are aware of some of these difficulties, you will be more able to face them together should you meet them. We pose here some of the questions which may arise.

My child was battered as a toddler. How do I explain that?

We are frequently asked how you tell a child potentially unpleasant things about his or her parents. It is easier to answer this by giving some examples of what you should **not** say:

Your birth mother loved you very much, but she did not have enough money to look after you because she had no job.

What happens then if either wage earner in a new family is made redundant? And how do you explain birth parents who are now working?

Your first mummy became ill, and that is why you came to live with us. But she still loves you.

What happens then when either you become ill or the birth mother gets better?

What may appear to be an act of kindness to protect the child is often an excuse to avoid a painful issue by the adult involved. The motto 'knowledge dispels fear' comes from a parachute school, but it is transferable to assisting a child to understand the past.

A child growing up in the love and security of a family would normally have knowledge and understanding of most of the events in that family's life. Not to have such information and knowledge can lead to confusion, unhappiness, misery.

There is often a very real sense of void. Some children have talked about a 'physical emptiness'; others about a 'knot' inside them. Knowledge can fill a void; understanding can dispel what is often an irrational fear and untie the knot. We know from adults who have been adopted as babies that to stumble upon the knowledge of their adoption in later life can have a devastating effect. The very foundation that their lives are built on can suddenly turn to sand. It is better to face reality gradually as a child and come to terms with it.

When your problem is how to explain why your child was battered, there is no easy solution, but lying about it won't help.

With the younger child, you need give little detail in the early stages, but gradually provide more detail in response to questions as the child gets older. Children often ask what they want to know, not what you want to tell them. Listen to the questions carefully and answer what the child has asked. Kay Donley says that the information given should be 'age appropriate'.

David had been removed from his mother's care because it was considered that she had neglected him. Yet she was neither bad nor wicked, more a victim of circumstances. Before we talked to David about this, we had obtained a family tree from her. From this, her own unhappy childhood came to light. She talked about struggling alone with David in a bedsitter, a 17-year-old with no help and little money.

Once we understood this, we talked together as a team about how we should explain events to David. This is what we told him:

Mary, your birth mum, had an unhappy childhood; she spent some time in a children's home herself. When you were born, she lived with her mother for a while, but decided to try to live in a bedsitter with you alone. She was all on her own without any help. Sometimes, because she was lonely, she went out and left you on your own. At other times, when you cried as all young children do, she smacked you too hard and bruised you. She was not a bad person, but did not know how to look after young children.

If children know that they can ask questions about the past freely throughout their childhood, you will have removed a major source of potential difficulty. The past will no longer be a mystery, not to be discussed. You will have brought it down to being normal, everyday and ordinary.

Children who have suffered many separations will blame themselves and believe that they are bad. If their parents were 'bad', it must mean they have inherited this 'badness'; they may even believe they were the cause of their parents' 'badness'. If you can help your child to understand the events and circumstances of the past, that will go a long way to healing the deep wounds of the hurt that has been suffered.

What if my child begins to lose interest in life story work?

From time to time during life story work, the child's interest will wane. Our descriptive illustrations in this book are only 'edited highlights'. We have spent many sessions when little progress seems to have been made. This need not be a problem.

There will be periods when nothing much is said or done during your sessions. If you are arriving at the same time each week or fortnight, you will have little control over what mood the child is in. If you force the pace, the life story work will become unpleasant for the child and that is not what you want. Of course, if the child is living with you, it is possible to choose moments to work together when the child wishes to respond, but even so there may be periods when the work is very slow.

All the time that you are helping a child, you need someone with whom to discuss events, and this is especially necessary when you are in the doldrums. There are some play techniques you can introduce after discussion with the colleagues and friends who are providing you with support (see Chapter 9).

What if my child regresses?

We have said already that during life story work, the child's behaviour may move backward until it is more appropriate to that of a younger child. You should be prepared for this. Regression can take a whole range and variety of forms. Bed wetting and soiling, temper tantrums, becoming quiet and withdrawn are just a few.

One 12-year-old boy insisted on being carried to bed each evening. Gradually this changed to being 'chased' to bed and, eventually, he went to bed 'normally'. During this period he also presented problems at school: shouting out in class, scribbling in his exercise books whenever his work was criticised. His foster carers regarded his developmental age at this period as being that of a six-year-old.

This regression is to be expected. It is a normal reaction. The movement backwards is usually shortlived and from it comes a healthy growth. It is important to know that your child may regress and that you may need help through difficult patches from other foster carers or your social worker, if you are the foster carer, or from colleagues if you are the worker involved.

Helping the child to talk about feelings

You will find as you work that the child will dictate the pace. Some of what is revealed will be distressing to both of you. If you are at a loss as to how to respond to this distress in words, physical affection or a sympathetic smile helps children to feel that you are on their side and are not put off by them or their past.

We have found that it is necessary from the beginning to establish that you are aware that the child has good/bad, happy/sad, and positive/negative feelings, and it is vital to establish that the child is aware that it is safe to talk about the bad as well as the good.

There are approaches which we have found useful in displaying that you accept these opposite emotions. Try to make it interesting and even enjoyable for children to express themselves by getting them to make things and draw pictures. We describe here how we have worked through pictures to help children to talk about feelings in a way that is safe for them. Violet Oaklander in her book *Windows to our Children* suggests and explains many useful ideas that can help children to express these emotions (see *Further Reading*).

Using questionnaires

A 'questionnaire' is a set of questions or unfinished sentences, like those shown in this illustration, which the child can answer, react to and discuss. A questionnaire can be useful in several ways in the early stages of working with a child on a life story.

I like my ....

I hate it when ....

I am afraid to ....

My face has a big smile when ....

I hate to eat ....

I hope that ....

Because of the structured nature of questionnaires, less demand is made on the child to be forthcoming and inventive. It is therefore particularly useful for children not used to writing down their thoughts or whose literacy is limited. For these children and for those who find it difficult to express themselves, for whatever reason, the questionnaire method can be used as a lead-in to producing a life story book or video, and could be included in the front of a life story book.

The structure of questionnaires is a matter of your choice. You can buy questionnaire booklets with attractive covers.*

Some of these are simply lists of questions progressing in sensitivity from fairly neutral questions, such as:

What is your favourite colour?
Which colour don't you like?

to progressively more sensitive questions, such as:

Who is your favourite person?
Who is your least favourite person?
Which person do you dislike most?

These questions lead children into making statements about themselves. They get them used to expressing both negative and positive statements about themselves and also convey the message that you are interested in them.

Some questionnaire books are structured differently and allow more creativity. They may contain, for example, a blank page with the heading, 'This is a picture of my favourite person' or 'This is how I see myself', thus encouriging children to draw pictures expressing aspects of themselves or their hopes and fears.

You can construct your own questionnaire encouraging the child to illustrate the cover with photos, drawings, elaborate writing or stick-on paper shapes. If you construct a questionnaire booklet yourself you can make it lead into areas which will be helpful for the child. One obvious idea is to omit negative statements altogether if you are working with a child who seems to have a wholly negative image of him or herself. Thus the questionnaire booklet when completed will contain only positive statements about the child.

Questionnaires can be structured to help a child to think about the future, with questions such as:

When I grow up I will live in ...
When I leave this children's home
I will feel ...
When I go to a new family, it will
help me to ...

The possibilities are endless. Don't forget, however, that questionnaires are only a method of eliciting information. They are not a substitute for life story work, which allows freer discussion and a wider ranging expression of views than questionnaires do by themselves.

In using questionnaires we avoid trying to interpret the answers back to the child. The answers to some questions may be very significant, or appear so, but to go into them in depth at an early stage would unsettle some children and might warn them off opening up and revealing their inner and private world. In other words, don't push too early.

Using pictures to enable a child to talk about feelings

Invite the child to draw a picture of him/herself and the things they like best which make them happy. Encourage them to write a caption to the picture about these happy/enjoyable events or to dictate such a caption for you to write. Try not to lead them or to search for any hidden meaning. Keep the activity simple and reproduce the child's own words.

*Got to be me! Merrill Harmin, Argus Communications, Niles, Illinois, USA, 1976

This is me! Merrill Harmin, Argus Communications, Niles, Illinois, USA, 1977

The Anti-Colouring Book, Susan Striker and Edward Kimmel, Scholastic Publications, London, 1978

I don't like going to bed.

Once this is completed to the child's satisfaction, suggest that he or she draws a picture of something they hate to do or which makes them angry. Usually children deny that anything makes them angry or sad, or that there is anything they hate. Often it has not been safe to show these feelings, so to deny them is normal. Don't push this issue.

Some children will respond with 'safe' dislikes. A six-year-old girl wrote 'I do not like those yellow things at school'. We later found that she meant the sweet corn occasionally served with school dinners. You might encourage a listing of 'safe' things that are hated, like cabbage, plums or 'those yellow things'.

All that you are doing at this stage is showing that you are aware that the child has both positive and negative feelings and that you accept both unconditionally. Sometimes there is resistance to drawing pictures, but we have successfully 'broken the ice' with the questionnaire method and the happy/sad face.

The happy/sad face

This face is made from two paper plates. One of them is cut in half and hinged to the back of the other so that it can be alternated.

The child – or you – can draw a happy face on the full plate. Then the half plate is turned over and either a sad or an angry face drawn on it. With this it is then possible to ask, 'Who are you today? Are you Miss Happy or Miss Sad?'

We have taken this further by asking the child to describe how 'the face' might be feeling inside. If the child can do this we write their comments on the

'feelings' cards (see below). You should avoid rushing this stage, especially if it is early in your work with the child.

'Feelings' cards

In order to express emotions, children need a repertoire of words which they feel comfortable using. Providing words to describe these feelings can be difficult, for the child will resist acknowledging that such emotions exist. Vera Fahlberg, in her film *Adoptive children, adaptive feelings*, demonstrates a technique she has developed; the use of 'feelings' cards. These are a set of cards each of which has a single word which identifies a specific emotional response.

We have taken this idea and used it with an individual child and with groups of children by making the initial introduction of these words into a game. The child (or children) is encouraged to call out words that describe an emotion and these words are written onto blank cards. The words may be, for example, good, bad, happy, sad, miserable, cheerful, kind, cruel. Once sufficient words have been gathered, the 'game' continues with the child drawing a face to match each 'feelings' word (see opposite).

This is a helpful exercise because it familiarises children with emotive words and gradually sensitises them to using these words to describe their feelings about situations and events. Introduced in this way, the potential threat and danger children may experience when attempts are made to attribute such feelings to them are avoided.

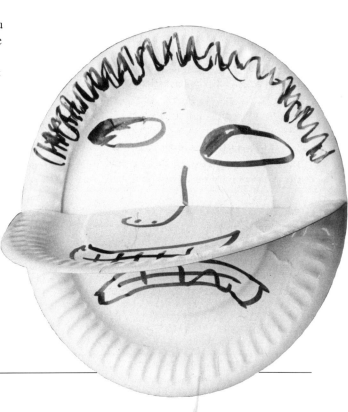

LOVE   SAD   GOOD

UNHAPPY WORRIED

UPSET   HAPPY   SURPRISED

For example, when you are later talking about an incident in the child's past, the cards can be laid out and the child can be encouraged to pick out a card that describes how they felt at the time. This method could be used when a child is describing how they felt at leaving a particular foster home and perhaps how they feel about it now. In this way past trauma can often be gradually resolved.

Throughout your work together, you can refer back to the cards from time to time and ask the child to add more words. A useful word is 'upset'. It covers a range of emotions and can be a substitute for a stronger emotion, such as 'angry' which the child may not be ready to use, especially in the early stages.

What will the child get from these sessions?

Don't be worried by what appears to be a lack of emotional response at this stage. Drawing the good/ bad pictures has an impact that will not become apparent until much later in life story work.

Avoid making any interpretation of the drawings, and accept a child's statement that they cannot think of anything that makes them upset. If they do disclose a small portion of their inner world, let it pass at this meeting, but make a note of it to be used as a reference point later. For example, when a child is starting to discuss feelings of loss, you might say, 'Do you remember when you drew a happy picture and could think of nothing that made you upset? I think that you feel upset because Anne lives with Mary, your 'born to' mother, and you do not.'

7

Some elements of a life story book

Visiting the past: taking children to visit places they have lived in or places they were familiar with, can help children begin to acknowledge the past.

There are various elements which may be included in a life story book. We list them here and then go on to discuss them in detail.

Where I came from	**My life graph**
My birth certificate	**Visiting the past**
My family tree	**Photographs about me**
My own map	

We illustrate how these elements work with some examples from the life story book of 'David' which he made with one of us some years ago when he was eight.

Where I came from

We used to assume that most children knew where babies come from. Now we know that this is not the case, and you will have to discover how much your child actually knows before you talk about this. Mother-and-baby books and health education books from either your local health centre or library should provide all the visual aids necessary to cover the period from conception to the first birthday.

David was, fortunately, aware that a baby grows in its mother's tummy, and from there it was a simple step to establish that he started to grow in Mary's (his born to mother) tummy when John planted his seed.

At this early stage, because photographs from relatives, foster carers and others may be slow to arrive, you will have to improvise, returning to fill in details later.

The hospital where the child was born will provide the time of birth and the weight at birth. You can give this information direct to the older child, but a younger child needs to be helped to understand it. The child can draw a clock face showing the time of birth and can stick in the book the equivalent of the birth weight in, say, pictures of bags of sugar.

The child can draw or collect pictures of very young children and give them captions. For example:

This is my drawing of a baby at six months. I might have looked like this.

I had my first birthday party at Oak Street where I lived with John and Mary, my born to dad and mum.

I grew in my mums tummy

When I was born I weighed 3.4 kilograms which is like 3 bags of Sugar

Granulated Sugar

My birth certificate

When we first started to do life story work with children, we provided a photocopy of their birth certificate to complete the part about their birth; we thought it would only be of passing interest to them. We were not prepared for the potent effect it had. Now we find it usually occupies a whole session. It is of immense interest to the children and can provoke numerous questions. Even small children who cannot read seem to grasp its significance to them, that it is documentary evidence that they were born and have an identity which can never be taken away from them.

At the same time the birth certificate can have a temporarily unsettling effect on adoptive parents and foster carers. For them, it is also documentary evidence that they are not the 'born to' parents of their child. If you are in this position remember that there is more to being a parent than giving birth and it is only if you are able to accept the facts of your child's birth that the child will feel accepted by you as his or her new parents.

Who's who

It is recognised now that the permanent, stable nuclear family is not the only family situation into which children are born and grow up. Whatever the arguments for and against this are, it certainly has the result that children have many more complex relationships to understand and adjust to than was once the case. It is not unusual for the family group to have siblings where the blood ties are only through one parent.

We need to remember that family situations do not remain static and that when a child leaves its family of origin, the parents may enter into new relationships where new partners bring with them their children. Further children may also be born into the new relationship so that the separated child acquires new half-siblings.

Not unnaturally, these situations may confuse the child with whom you are working and arouse feelings of envy or resentment towards those siblings who have stayed, or been born into, the family of origin.

It is often helpful to explore these feelings in a group setting, where all the children have similar backgrounds (see also Chapter 11, *Working with groups*). This helps a child to understand that their family situation is not abnormal, and their feelings and possible confusions are shared by other children in the same situation.

The Children Act emphasises partnership with significant people in a child's life. Similarly, moves towards open adoption signal a greater understanding of adoption as a life-long process, where adopted people need to know and understand their origins, and may work to maintain links with their birth family. It is important for a child to understand the nature of their relationship with all the people in their family of origin, and if possible, their whereabouts and current situation.

In our counselling of adults who were adopted as children, we have been faced time and time again with the anger and hurt that can result from an adult discovering that they have brothers and sisters whose existence was kept secret from them whilst they were children.

Ecomaps (see page 38), family trees and diagrams of blood ties have all proved useful as ways of explaining a child's relationship to siblings, half-siblings and significant adults in their family of origin.

We live in an era of serial monogamy in which one in three marriages end in divorce. Many people enter into relationships which are stable and in which they have children. Some of these relationships eventually end too. As the years progress, there may be a tangled network of full siblings, half-siblings and stepsiblings. It should be remembered that these family networks are neither abnormal nor unusual and it is important for children to understand this. We have found that looking at the complexity of family ties can be usefully incorporated when working with children in groups (see page 48). In doing so, children can become aware that although their lives are unique there are similarities with the experiences of other children. The Children Act emphasises the importance of family links, regrettably all too frequently ignored in the past. For example, if David's father and paternal grandparents had been approached at the time he was removed from his birth mother's care perhaps his life would have run a different course.

We have developed the following illustration from our work with children to help them, and us, understand how the family network has emerged and how the blood ties developed. Although we have attempted to keep this illustration very simple it demonstrates that family ties quickly become complicated and difficult to understand once they break the commonly

perceived mould of a married couple with two children. It is worth repeating that this concept of family life, regularly portrayed in the media, particularly on television, is in reality a myth and the model drawn here is perhaps closer to the norm than most of us realise.

Mary and Kevin met when they were 17 years old.

Mary became pregnant and gave birth to Wayne. Kevin was Wayne's father. Kevin said he was too young to marry and he and Mary drifted apart. Mary often visited Kevin's mother (Wayne's grandmother) with Wayne.

When Wayne was two years old, Mary met Pete and they started to go out together.

Pete had lived with Alison for five years and they had two children, Annie and Cheryl. Pete and Alison had stopped living together about six months before Pete met Mary.

Pete and Mary married in May 1980. Pete became Wayne's stepfather.

Pete and Mary had two children, Lisa and Alan.

Mary told Wayne that Lisa and Alan were his 'half' brother and sister.

Annie and Cheryl were Lisa and Alan's half-sisters and Wayne's stepsisters.

Below we show what the family links would look like.

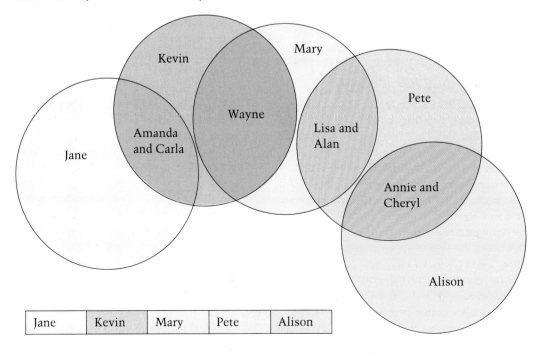

Jane	Kevin	Mary	Pete	Alison

(The colours, and the way in which they blend, are used to identify the blood ties. Children may need assurance that they did not have to have a 'blood tie' to a significant adult to be loved. Sadly, for Wayne, it was used to help him understand why Pete treated him differently and eventually rejected him.)

Meanwhile, Kevin, Wayne's father, had married and had two children, Carla and Amanda. Wayne used to see his half-siblings at his grandparents (Kevin's parents).

Understanding these family links and ties is an essential requirement of the Children Act 1989 which stresses keeping children in contact with relatives, especially grandparents and siblings, as well as birth parents. It is through helping the child understand these relationships, talking to the child and establishing what is significant for the child, that we will be able to engage the child in decisions about contact.

In the past, when parental contact with the child has been terminated, this has almost automatically included siblings, grandparents and significant adults, such as aunts and uncles. Evidence from counselling adults who had been separated from siblings in childhood suggests that they feel robbed of these childhood experiences.

Planning for children under the Children Act requires a comprehensive assessment. Using the 'family ties graph', the family tree graph and the life graph can be an important element in such an assessment. The Act states clearly that children are best cared for in their own families. If on completing all this work, it is not possible for the child to be cared for in his or her own family, then this work can be used as a basis for understanding why this is not possible.

My family tree

As we have said, the birth family is the best source of information for making a family tree. We consider that its making, and showing the child his or her place on it, is very important.

Knowledge of the extended family can be painful to children because it emphasises that they are severed from their birth family and forebears. Nonetheless it can also do a great deal to help children understand some of the events that led to the loss of their family.

By working on his family tree Jimmy, a nine-year-old, could start to understand why he came to be looked after as a two-year-old, bruised and neglected. He understood that his mother was sixteen years old when he was born, and that she too had been 'in care'.

Jimmy was living in a large children's home in which there were several sixteen-year-old girls. He began to grasp that his mother was not bad or cruel, just very young and ill-prepared to be a mother to him.

Remember that family patterns are now diverse and it may help children to accept their own situations to know that there are such variations. One marriage in three ends in divorce and one child in five lives in a single parent family. Life story work should not, therefore, attempt to portray a model of family life that is alien to the child and removed from the varying patterns that exist in society.

David's mother, as you can see from his family tree (overleaf), entered into three relationships before she established a stable life for herself. Frequently children come from such changing households with further developments occurring after they have left. These complicated relationships can be an additional source of stress for a child because the changes are difficult to understand.

If the plans are to resettle children back in their birth families, it is important to ensure they have a knowledge and understanding of the changes that have gone on since they left. If the child is not returning to the birth family and the changes in the family are one of the reasons for this, the child needs to understand why. For instance, David was angry because his half-sister Lisa lived with his mother and he did not. There had been an unsuccessful attempt to settle him back with his mother, but the changes in his family meant that they could not assimilate an older child.

My own map

This is a device we use to provide the child with a sense of movement through time. Along with the child we map the moves of the birth family and the child's own moves since leaving them. Often we start with the geographical area where the birth mother was born and lived. This map may help a child to understand part of his or her own predicament if, for example, the birth mother had an unstable childhood with many moves too (see example overleaf).

When working together on a 'map', it is important to remember that a child who has lived apart from his or her family of origin will have a different concept of time to your own. We have found that a child can conceptualise the length of the last school holiday and you can build on this. However, if you say, 'You lived for two years with your mother in this town', it is likely to mean very little.

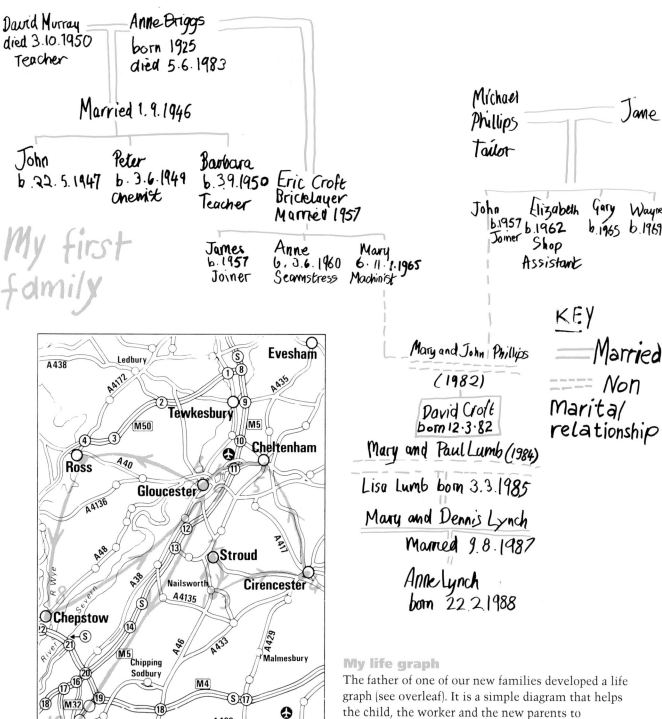

David Murray
died 3.10.1950
Teacher

Anne Briggs
born 1925
died 5.6.1983

Married 1.9.1946

John
b. 22.5.1947

Peter
b. 3.6.1949
Chemist

Barbara
b. 3.9.1950
Teacher

Eric Croft
Bricklayer
Married 1957

James
b. 1957
Joiner

Anne
b. 3.6.1960
Seamstress

Mary
6.11.1.1965
Machinist

My first family

Michael
Phillips
Tailor

Jane

John
b.1957
Joiner

Elizabeth
b.1962
Shop
Assistant

Gary
b.1965

Wayne
b.1969

Mary and John Phillips
(1982)

David Croft
born 12.3.82

Mary and Paul Lumb (1984)

Lisa Lumb born 3.3.1985

Mary and Dennis Lynch
Married 9.8.1987

Anne Lynch
born 22.2.1988

KEY

═══ Married

==== Non
Marital
relationship

A map can help provide the child with a sense of movement through time.

My life graph

The father of one of our new families developed a life graph (see overleaf). It is a simple diagram that helps the child, the worker and the new parents to understand the movements in the child's life. When we started using the life graph, we found resistance from children to working in what we saw as a logical order, from birth to the present day. To the children this was not logical. For them it was simpler to work back through time, starting from the present. David chose to leave the painful recent past till last (see overleaf).

Again, you can write the entries in pencil for the child to ink over. Using different pens for colour-coding the different types of care (with birth parents, with foster carers, etc) can clarify the graph.

```
12TH MARCH - BORN IN MATERNITY HOSPITAL  6 P.M.         1983
I LIVED WITH MARY, MY BORN TO MOTHER, AND
GRANDMOTHER CROFT. WE LIVED AT 117 OAK STREET

MY FIRST BIRTHDAY PARTY                                 1983
5TH JUNE. GRANDMOTHER CROFT DIED

3RD NOVEMBER. HIGH MEADOW NURSERY

MY SECOND BIRTHDAY                                      1984
5TH MAY. WITH MARY AT 117 OAK STREET

28TH DECEMBER. LEAKE STREET CHILDREN'S HOME             1985
3RD MARCH. LISA LUMB BORN
MY THIRD BIRTHDAY
3RD JUNE. WITH MARY AND PAUL LUMB
        - EASTWOOD ROAD
20TH NOVEMBER. THE CHILDREN'S HOSPITAL
5TH JANUARY. THE HOLLIES CHILDREN'S HOME
MY FOURTH BIRTHDAY                                      1986

24TH DECEMBER. PETER AND JOAN BATT. FOSTER PARENTS      1987
MY FIFTH BIRTHDAY

9TH AUGUST. MARY MARRIES DENNIS LYNCH

22ND FEBRUARY. ANNE LYNCH BORN                          1988
MY SIXTH BIRTHDAY

29TH MAY. MARY AND DENNIS LYNCH, DUNCAN TERRACE         1989

5TH JANUARY. MOVED WITH FAMILY TO NEWTOWN GATE
2ND FEBRUARY. THE HAVEN CHILDREN'S HOME                 1990
30TH MAY. EASTFIELD ASSESSMENT CENTRE

                                                        1991
12TH NOVEMBER  WITH CHRIS AND EDDIE
```

and troubled. Younger children who cannot yet read or write, can be encouraged to colour each segment of time. We find that this helps them to understand time and events. Birthdays are useful for marking the passage of time, especially if there are occasions about which the child may have happy memories.

The 'life graph' is also valuable in predicting when possible setbacks may occur during the year; the anniversary effect. Claudia Jewett Jarratt, an American child and family therapist, believes that children can become unsettled for what appears to be unexplained reasons. She puts this down to the fact that some trauma may have occurred in the child's past and when the time in the year that it happened comes round again, this unsettling incident can cause problems in the present. Claudia Jewett Jarratt attributes this to the child's in-built clock being linked to the seasons of the year and the daylight hours which then trigger the response. It is often possible, therefore, to predict when unsettling events may occur. For example, David had suffered two traumatic and distressing experiences in the month of March. These events were separated by a gap of five years but following the second trauma, his carers noticed that around this period of the year, David was reluctant to attend school and, in fact, developed an illness which was not feigned, having to stay off school for several days with a heavy cold. When this pattern emerged, it was possible to help David understand that traumas in the past were emerging into and distorting his present. His carers found it helpful to look at his life story book again and talk about these events. As he grew older and gained more life experience it increased his ability to understand and place in context what had happened.

The life graph can be varied to suit the needs of the child. We know of foster carers who have prepared a life graph of the birth parents too, so that the child can understand what was happening to them as well.

Visiting the past

Many children deny that events in their past have happened. The uncompleted sections on the life graph may indicate to you where their problems lie. If you are satisfied that children like this are familiar with many aspects of the life graph, we believe that taking them on a trip to visit all the places they have lived in can help to overcome this difficulty.

Such visits will entail careful preparation, not only of the child, but also of the people from the past, and must be carefully timed. It should never be a substitute for the actual life story work but an accompaniment to it. If we can accomplish the visits in one day, we do so. The preparations will take longer

On the way through the life graph there will be painful events which children will want to avoid talking about in the early stages, but will eventually come to them when they are feeling stronger and more secure. We always prepare life graphs in pencil and introduce them when we are talking about the child's birth, suggesting that they ink over that first entry. In the next session, the child inks in the last entry, which is the present day. From there, we ask them to ink in any section they wish and we talk about this section together.

At first most children will only be prepared to consider the less troubled periods of their lives, so do not expect any startling revelations. As the child inks over the 'safe' periods, the uncompleted parts will indicate the periods about which they are unhappy and the work involved invariably means that the journey will have to be arranged by the child's social worker, who may need to make preliminary visits in order to prepare and explain the purpose of the contact.

The child's safety must also be considered in planning visits to the past, especially in cases of undisclosed sexual abuse. Workers and carers need to be sensitive to the possibility of such visits reawakening repressed memories for traumatised children. The visits may also prompt some children to disclose experiences they were unable to remember.

Whenever possible on these trips, work backward from the present using the child's life graph and personal map. This physical and geographical tracing of the child's life assists and enables them to place their life in context. It is invaluable in assisting you too, and it is inevitably a moving experience for all concerned.

An unexpected bonus for us has been the warmth, affection and welcome received at each stopping place. Often children may have left these places abruptly, believing they have harmed and damaged people. To discover that they have not can be a relief and, therefore, an additional dividend.

At a later stage when 'bridging' children into the future (see page 35) and using the candle technique (see page 36), we are able to refer back to this journey and to the positive benefits to the children of having people in their past who loved them.

We also use these trips to simulate photographs of earlier events, which are then captioned in the life story book.

How these visits help children to begin to acknowledge their past and to face up to painful events in their lives showed clearly with David. He had denied any knowledge of the time he spent at High Meadow Nursery even when he was taken there. For him to admit he had lived there was to acknowledge that his mother had been unable to care for him adequately. The cook and matron remembered him with affection and told tales of his early childhood – normally the function of parents. Afterwards, David walked upstairs and into a bedroom, and said: 'That was my bed and I used to watch the trains from that window.'

Photographs about me

Photographs are an invaluable and essential part of life story work. They are not only a record of past events but also a means by which a child may be able to talk about the past and express feelings about it. However, you must avoid the trap of turning life story work into simply producing a photograph album with captions. The photographs are there to provide you with a focus for working together. We suggest that you may, alongside making a book or video, help the child to make a separate album of photographs. A photograph can be stuck on to a blank sheet of paper and used alongside the life graph and family tree. The child can write captions to the photo which link their knowledge of all three components.

Photographs can provide an invaluable record of past events and help a child express feelings.

Although children will be interested in the photographs, they may be reluctant to use the sensitive ones in a life story book. David asked to keep the photograph of his birth mother and was allowed to do so, but we retained copies too as we were uncertain about whether or not he would destroy the others because they raised such painful memories.

David dictated under a photograph taken at Christmas 1989:

I spent Christmas with my mum, Lisa, Anne and Dennis at New Town Estate. Lisa and Anne got bikes and I got a toy car. It's not fair, Lisa and Anne live with my mum and I don't. Dennis is okay, he used to give me rides on his motorbike. My mum used to shout and hit me with a belt. It's not fair Mr Hughes and the staff at Eastfield keep me from going home to my mum. I hate them. When I was with my mum I jumped on the settee and made a hole in it.

David dictated at another session:

August 1984. This is me on a donkey at Filey. I went with my mum, Lisa, Uncle James and Paul Lumb for the day. My mum was not a bad person. She was not good looking after little ones.

The photographs of his mother had a deep emotional impact, but he eventually placed them in his life story book and dictated, 'Mary wants me to be adopted but I want Mary to adopt me.'

At the following session he dictated:

This is my first mum Mary and my dog. She gave the dog away. It made me sad because she gave the dog away. It makes me sad because I cannot live without her.

David's captions show how photographs help a child to talk about and express feelings. Certain photographs will be more significant because of the importance the child attaches to them. For example, we spent two sessions on the three photographs of David's mother, whereas seven pictures of his foster carers were dealt with in half a session. The reason for this was that the photographs of David's mother provided a means of discussing his relationship with her, the hurt he felt at not living with her and a movement towards realising that to return to her was not possible. It was a start at helping him to understand that his mother cared about him even though her circumstances meant she could not care for him.

David was obviously pleased with all his photographs

and wanted to show them and share them with his friends. This raised another problem. His life story book contained information which was personal and confidential, not for general consumption. How could he share the photographs but not the information? We asked ourselves how our own children did this: the answer was by using the family album. David was provided with a separate album to share.

Videos about me

Easy to use video cameras make possible the inclusion of video recordings in life story work, either to be included in a book, or as the complete story, or for use in the work to help children come to terms with their past. The impact of a videoed interview with a parent, relative or family friend will be great. If a parent wants to give an explanation why they could not cope at the time the child separated from them, but could not face talking to the child direct, they can do so on video film.

Similarly, if previous neighbours want to describe the birth family or remember their experiences of the child, they can do so on video film for the child to keep. A film of a previous house, or foster family, or children's home will be more immediate than photographs. Cine film can be transformed on to video film so that old holiday films or films of babies and children can be kept by the child. More and more video recordings are being kept by families and can be copied for the child to keep. A creative teenager, with appropriate preparations, can even go off to make their own video recordings (yes, they usually bring the camera back!) of past places and people. The use of video films can considerably enhance life story work in all sorts of ways and will be worth considering whenever this work is undertaken.

Thomas, Mary and Nellie: their life story book

This case study shows how the life story book with its visits and photographs worked for one child.

Thomas was 13 years old when he was placed with Mary, a single woman in her late 40s and her widowed mother. It was his ninth placement and he came direct to them from his third foster home breakdown. Thomas' parents had separated before he was born. His mother, who already had one child, was estranged from the extended family and without help or support. She left Thomas in the hospital where he was born, believing he would be adopted. Thomas was placed with elderly foster carers and stayed with them for eight years until he was removed because he was refusing to go to school. What follows is an account of how we untangled and came to understand Thomas' past through a life story book.

Thomas wrote in his life story book, 'My first foster mother, who I thought was my real mum, used to spoil me. She let me do anything. We used to tie sheets together and play at Tarzan. The social worker took me on holiday because I asked him if he would. He took me to a children's home. I was upset when I found out I was not going back to my foster mother.'

It was very difficult to make Thomas' life story book because we had photographs only from his first foster home and one photograph taken in a children's home when he was ten years old. Very little was known about his birth parents. There was only one thing to do: visit the area around the south coast where he had spent most of his life and experienced three foster homes and five children's homes. This Mary, Thomas and I, as his social worker, did, starting with the maternity hospital where he was born.

Thomas wrote afterwards, *My mum asked me if I would like to go to my home town to see all my old friends and children's home which I had stayed in. I am happy at home with my mum, grandma and the dogs. There are lots of things that have happened that I would rather like to forget, but I did want to show mum and grandma where I used to play, the shops, park and seaside.'*

Mary wrote too, *'I was surprised that Thomas could remember so much about the area, he seemed to know where every street and road came out – Thomas had come to life, this was where he had enjoyed himself as a young lad. I could not help but feel happy for him as we strolled around hand in hand.'*

The day was exhausting, enjoyable and rewarding. Move after move, yet Thomas was welcomed back with genuine affection at each place we visited. Mary said afterwards that it laid to rest a lot of ghosts: it helped her to understand and become closer to Thomas but it also made her feel angry at what had happened to her 'son'.

After this the next major step did not seem so big. I traced and visited Jane, his birth mother, who had last seen him as a baby. Taking my camera with me I explained about Thomas's life story book and she willingly allowed me to photograph her. In exchange I gave her recent photographs of Thomas. Jane was now re-married with two children, her oldest child living with her first husband. She also provided detailed information about her own family and I was able to give this to Thomas for his life story book.

The next step was to arrange a meeting between Thomas and Mary with Jane and her second husband and family. This was done and, at the same time, Jane signed her consent for Mary to adopt Thomas. This meeting, which was fraught with potential risks, went smoothly from the moment Thomas produced his life story book to show Jane. From there, a meeting was arranged with Graham, Thomas' birth father, and Mary and Thomas. Again, information was provided for Thomas' family tree: he had been named after Graham's younger brother. Graham, too, signed the consent to the adoption application.

(It should be stressed that these meetings were only arranged after all the participants clearly understood the purpose. At no time was it to test out whether Thomas could be reunited with his birth parents. It was for Thomas' sake to dispel any secret dreams and fears he might have had about them and to free him emotionally from his past.)

Fifteen months after Thomas went to live with Mary, she adopted him. Two months after this Mary allowed him to spend a week with Jane and her family. (Mary enjoyed not having to ask a social worker for permission.) The following week Mary and 'gran' Nellie collected Thomas and his half-brother and sister and took them to spend a week with Graham, who now lives with his parents and his elder son.

For the first time in his life Thomas is enjoying school, self-assured, confident and secure in the knowledge that Mary loves him. We rarely talk about the past now: there is too much happening in the present and much to look forward to in the future.

8

Bridging: past, present and future

We use the term 'bridging' for the time when we link the past and the present and provide a bridge to the future. We have slowly, from our own experience, come to the conclusion that successfully 'bridging' children is a crucial factor in them remaining in their permanent substitute family.

In doing the life story work together, you will have gained unique insight and information about the child's past. This will prove invaluable in preparing the new family before the child arrives. Moving to a new family or returning to a birth family is a stressful time for children and they need help and support to cross the 'bridge'. It is a time when past, present and future can be placed in context and 'ghosts' and fantasies laid to rest.

Vera Fahlberg suggests, and we too have found, that a child about to move into a new family is in a state of aroused anxiety. But it is often possible to deal with earlier unresolved attachment and separation feelings by talking about a child's life experiences through life story work.

Kay Donley considers that appropriate bridging messages should be incorporated throughout life story work. She has identified the task, at this stage and in the early stages of placement, as one of disengaging

the child from significant parental figures in the past, usually the birth mother, and assisting the child to engage with the 'new' mother. Vera Fahlberg describes the process as one of obtaining 'emotional permission' in order that the child can attach him or herself to the new family. Within the child's experiences there will be a hierarchy of people, starting with the birth mother, who can signal the message of disengagement and start the process of emotional permission to move towards a new family.

At this important stage, it is essential to re-read a child's life story book to make sure that you have not overlooked clues about hidden anxieties and worries. For instance, it became evident that the various statements David had written about his mother indicated a strong attachment to her which was a mixture of reality and fantasy. His life story book contained several questionnaires and within these David had specifically mentioned his mother. For example:

The person I most like – *my mother*

My face has a big smile when – *I see my mother*

Things I worry about – *my mother*

I would not like to live without – *my mother*

David's birth mother had provided information and photographs of his early life. She had been involved in the plans to place him with an adoptive family and had stated she would consent to his adoption. Through her involvement in helping with material for David's life story book, the concept of disengagement and emotional permission was explained to her. When David had lived with his new family for nine months, a 'farewell' meeting was arranged. At this meeting his mother 'signalled' her approval of David's new parents. David was aware that his mother had consented to his adoption and given her 'permission' for him to attach himself to his new family.

It is not always possible to involve birth parents in this way either because they cannot be found or because they are unwilling to participate. Kay Donley suggests that you go to the next person in the child's hierarchy. This might be either a previous foster carer or another adult with whom the child has made a significant relationship, such as a member of staff in a children's home. She believes that a child's social worker does not have this significance.

Saying 'hello' and 'goodbye'

Since the publication of *Making Life Story Books*, we have heard Claudia Jewett Jarratt talk about the importance of saying 'hello' and 'goodbye'. We suggest that work is to be done in conjunction with the use of 'life graphs' described on page 30.

Typically, a child, before being looked after, may have had several moves already and will possibly experience several moves between, for example, children's homes and foster carers. Many of these moves will have been made in a crisis, unplanned and regrettably unexplained. This may have been the case while the child was living with his or her own family, and almost certainly when the child started to be looked after away from the family, and the chance to say 'goodbye' properly was lost.

In a child's memory, the moves become a blur and events run into each other. This can be damaging and add to the child's lack of confidence and impair a child's sense of identity. If you are working with a child towards a move from, for example, a temporary foster home to an adoptive family, it presents a golden opportunity to rework some of the earlier experiences which might have been traumatic.

We describe the well established candles ritual and nowadays we can enhance this by introducing other 'hello' and 'goodbye' rituals. For example, if a child is leaving a temporary foster carer to move to a permanent new family, we encourage the foster carer to hold a farewell party. Similarly, if the child is

moving school, due to changing families, we encourage the school to ritualise this by formally recognising the child's departure. These ritualised endings are especially important if the child has made significant attachments during a stay with a family or in a children's home.

An 'Advent' or 'Moving' Calendar

Once children learn that a decision has been made for them either to return to their birth family or be introduced to a new family, their anxiety level rises. One reason for this, we believe, is that children feel that these plans are outside their control. The process of moving therefore becomes frightening and confusing. We have found that making what we call an 'Advent' or 'Moving' calendar can reduce the uncertainty that may surround the move.

An Advent calendar has doors and windows that open to reveal aspects of the Christmas season during the 'countdown' period to Christmas Day. In the same way the doors in a 'Moving' calendar open up during the 'countdown' to a placement. Usually visits home or to a new family are planned over several weeks during the period of introductions. The doors in the 'Moving' calendar display a date. When they open they reveal a certain amount of specific information. On the opposite page is an example of what such a calendar might reveal.

The candles ritual

The candles ritual is a way, at this stage, of 'bridging' or demonstrating to children that they have the capacity to love people. Children enjoy rituals and they can be used to help understand a particular idea. We borrowed the candle technique from Claudia Jewett Jarratt, who describes it in her book, *Adopting the Older Child*. We have used it on many occasions because it demonstrates to the child that not only have they the capacity to love, but that it is also safe to love others.

A row of candles is used to represent all the people the child has loved in his or her life. In front of this row, you place a candle to symbolise the child. While lighting this candle, you explain that it represents the child's birth, when he or she came into the world with an inborn ability to love people. Next, if it is significant, you light the first candle representing the birth mother and explain that this was the first person the child loved. You continue the process down the line, lighting a candle for each new situation the child moved into and each new person who was loved. Tell the child that because they were born with the ability to love people, it is not necessary to put out (extinguish) the love of the previous carer before loving another.

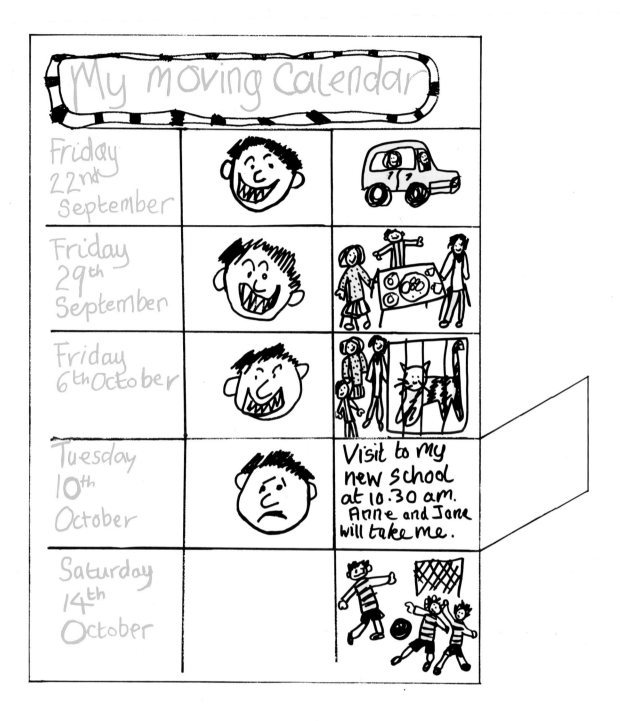

This technique illustrates how important it is to keep love alive. Usually we only use it when a new family is imminent, for it reveals that it is safe for the child to light the candles belonging to the new family. Once the child is with the new family, we repeat the ritual with the new parents to emphasise how important it is not to extinguish the love the child has for others from the past.

Perhaps David best summed up the experience when he said, 'The candles I have just lit for Christine and Eddie (his new parents) are burning the brightest and Mary's (his birth mother) candle, lit first, is burning down and will gradually fade away.'

Six months later, David's relationship with his new mother was showing signs of strain. She was able to discuss this with him by reminding him of the candle ritual, commenting that perhaps he felt he had been let down by mother figures in the past and now he was afraid to light a candle for her. David was eventually able to recognise this and accept her assurance that it was safe to light her candle.

A child's responses to the question 'Why am I here?' will help you to perceive his or her understanding of their situation. You can then refer to the life story work you have done together to discuss the significant people in the child's life and illustrate their present relationship and the type of contact they have. For example:

My birth mum – writes me letters and speaks to me on the telephone

My social worker – telephones me and visits me

After David had been living with his new family for three months, he began to have behavioural problems at school which led to him being threatened with exclusion. We used David's ecomap to arrive at an understanding of how his behaviour at school was threatening his future with his new family. On the line from his new home to school he drew arrows attacking it, but shortly after this the extremes of his behaviour subsided and whilst difficulties remained for a time, the threat of exclusion was removed.

The 'three parents'

We always use Vera Fahlberg's 'three parents' as a means of helping children during the bridging period. It has many uses, for example, demonstrating to children that it is not possible to take away from them what was given to them at birth by their parents.

Below is an extract from her book, *Helping Children when they must Move*.

(Note that she uses the term 'foster care' in the American sense, to include both foster care and residential care.)

We believe that much too often children are not told about what is happening to them when they are moved. Foster care may seem familiar and logical to social workers but makes no sense to children. We have developed a method of explaining foster care to children. The idea is to explain the role of the various parents in their lives and to outline who is responsible for what. We draw three circles (like those opposite) and give the child an explanation of the different roles of each kind of parent.

The Children Act, with its emphasis on parental responsibility, and the possibility of shared parental responsibility, has affected the concept of Vera Fahlberg's 'three parents', especially the 'legal parent'. Nonetheless, despite the changes, we have retained it in this edition because we regard it as a useful method not only of helping children to understand what has happened to them but, with the increased

The ecomap

Vera Fahlberg in *Helping Children when they must Move** describes what is called an ecomap, originally developed as an initial interviewing tool to open communication between the child and social worker. It shows the child and the various people, places and concerns which form a part of his or her life. Children can discuss these elements and how they relate to them and so gain further understanding of their life as a whole and why they are where they are.

We have successfully taken this idea and adapted it for use not only during the bridging period but also when the child is in the new home. Then it becomes a means of helping the child and the new family to understand in pictorial form what we believe is happening. Vera Fahlberg considers it works best with children in the five to twelve age range, but we have used it as effectively with older children.

*Vera Fahlberg acknowledges the work of Marietta Spencer of the Children's Home Society of Minnesota for this idea.

involvement of birth parents it serves to help them to understand the legal and emotional aspects too. We have now modified the 'three parents' and it looks like this:

BIRTH PARENT

PARENT WITH LEGAL RESPONSIBILITY

LOOKING AFTER CARER

Despite the legislative changes the emotional aspects remain unchanged for the child, especially the strong feelings about his or her birth parents and the confusion of being parted from them. The terminology and/or precise application of the underlying concept may need to be altered to meet the precise circumstances of the child (eg whether he or she is in care or accommodated) and whether or not the placement is with adoptive parents. What is important is that the child (and the child's birth parents) have a right to an understandable explanation of how they fit

into the legal framework, but there is a corresponding right to understand that their birth endowment remains unchanged for life and that no-one can either alter this or take it away; it is a fact of their very existence.

Vera Fahlberg continues:

We say that every birth has parents. There can be no changes in birth parents. Each child has one birth mother and one birth father, no one can ever do anything to change this situation. All children in our society also have legal parents. The legal parent makes the major decisions in a child's life. The parenting parent is the person who is available on a day-to-day basis to meet the child's needs for nurture and discipline.

For many children, one set of parents are simultaneously the birth parents, the legal parents and the parenting parents. However, in foster care and adoption these different kinds of jobs are split up.

Birth parent

Life itself
Sex
Physical looks
Intellectual potential
Predisposition for certain
diseases
Basic personality type
(such as shy, stubborn,
active)

Parenting parent

Love
Provides food, toys, clothes
Gives hugs and kisses
Disciplines
Takes care of you when sick

Legal parent

Financial responsibility
Safety and security
Where you live
Where you go to school
Sign for operations
Permission to travel abroad
Sign for marriage under age
Sign for going into services
under age

These diagrams are based on Vera Fahlberg's 'three parents'.

The child in care still has a set of birth parents. In the case of voluntary reception into care, the legal parent may still be the birth parent, or the legal parenting role may be shared by the birth parent and the agency. For example, the birth parent's signature might be required for an adolescent to join the army, while the agency might have the right to select the home in which the child lives and the school the child attends.

When parental rights have been terminated by the court, an agency or the court becomes the legal parent. When the child is fostered, the foster parents are the parenting parents. When there are disputes about who should be the legal parent and who should be the parenting parent, a court makes the decision.

When a child returns to the birth home, but the agency continues to have legal custody, the diagram can help explain responsibilities. The birth parent then is the parenting parent and the birth parent, but aspects of the legal parent role are retained in the agency or the court.

If parental rights are terminated, the child continues to have the same birth parents; he has the agency or court as a legal parent and has foster parents as the parenting parent. When we explain adoption to such a child, we tell him that termination means no one set of parents will again fill all three parenting roles; however, adoption allows us to combine two aspects of parenting – the legal parent and the parenting parent – in one set of parents. The child learns that social workers or courts will no longer make decision about him; but rather that the set of parents with whom he lives will also be in charge of making the major decisions in his life.

In all cases this method of explanation accepts the fact that the child has a set of birth parents. The acceptance of birth parents and what they mean in a child's life is critical if we are to help children deal with their feelings about separation from birth parents.

Life story work as a reference point

Life does not run smoothly, so you can expect even a well-prepared child to present problems in the new setting. Most of these will be normal behaviour, but occasionally inappropriate behaviour may have its origins in earlier life experiences, for example, David's fear of loving Chris, his adoptive mother. Vera

Fahlberg likens the process to that of a telephone switchboard where the child's past becomes plugged into their present and begins to interfere with and distort it. Life story work may help to identify what has led to this problem and a life story book can be used, at a time of crisis, as a reference point.

Life story work and the way it is documented represents a point of view based on information that was available at the time the work was undertaken. It is important that neither you nor the child regards the work as static or complete simply because a book is produced. Life experiences and the normal developmental process mean that past experiences will be re-examined in light of new ones.

Julie, an eleven-year-old girl, was having difficulties settling into her new family and her new parents were having difficulty adjusting to her too. It was possible to turn to her life story book, where similar incidents had occurred, and use it as a reference to the difficulties of living in a family. Julie was struggling with assimilating herself into her new family. She had experienced two foster home breakdowns and she was becoming anxious that her third placement was about to disrupt. It was by helping her express these fears and linking them to painful events in her past that she could begin to understand how her past was interfering with her present. Julie then wrote the following:

I want to stay with Margery and John and for them to be my mum and dad. It is hard to build up a new family. When I fell out with my mum and dad I felt upset. He said if I don't change my attitude I will have to go. I want to change my attitude. When I quarrel with my mum it makes me feel miserable. It makes me worried because I might have to leave home. I would like to stay with mum and dad because it is the right place to be. There is nowhere else to go really. I want to co-operate with other people but it is hard to understand how to do this. I got on with my dad alright and I love them both. I won't go on being miserable and having no friends. I don't understand why I can't make friends because I had friends at Eastfield Lodge.

We were able to show this to her new parents and the tension noticeably reduced. Her new parents were able to understand that Julie's behaviour was not deliberate but was brought about by anxieties from her past that had leaked into her present.

9

Beyond life story work

For some children, life story work will not be sufficient to penetrate the barrier they have erected to protect their inner and painful world. We have found this particularly with children who have experienced numerous moves which have severely damaged their ability to form and sustain relationships beyond a superficial level. Such children have been called 'emotionally frozen'. Vera Fahlberg defines this as having an over-investment in the past, into which all energies seem to go, creating an emotional imbalance.

The trauma of separation from the birth parent is probably the worst any child will ever experience. Its effects should never be under-estimated or ignored, even if many years have passed. Children may become fixated or 'emotionally frozen' as a result of being separated, and the risk of breakdown in a permanent family placement is very high because their shallowness seems to invite rejection. After several placements such children begin to attract 'labels' which state that they are immature, superficial in relationships, indiscriminate in affection, self-centred and so on.

You will have noticed from David Croft's life graph that he had nine moves in seven years, and was just such an 'emotionally frozen' child. Children like

David hardly ever feel able to talk in an adult way about themselves. They need to find other ways of 'talking' and we need to find other ways of talking to them. There are lots of different methods, but essentially they are all based on the sort of communication that children themselves favour: using play as a means of communication and a means of working out the situation.

Communication through play
What follows is not about advanced techniques, but suggested ways of communicating with children which we have used successfully. Anyone who has seen children being parents to their dolls and copying their parents' ways of talking will realise that this is a good way for us to get through to children. To do this makes demands on us as adults, because it requires us to shed our inhibitions. We must enter the world of the child whilst being sensitive to what the child might be saying and being ready to respond accordingly.

We have used these 'communication through play' techniques with children from three to fifteen years old. As we have gained confidence in using them, we have introduced these techniques into our preparation of the life story book rather than at the end, and now we often use play before we start life story work.

Glove puppets

Having one glove puppet to speak for you and another for the child to speak through is a useful way to talk with children of all ages, but is particulary useful with younger children. No matter how good a relationship you have with a child, most find difficulty in revealing their inner world. They feel safer disclosing their intimate thoughts through puppets because of the distance the puppet seems to provide. Usually a two-way conversation can be started by your puppet asking the child's puppet questions.

The following is a conversation between a foster carer and Susan, a five-year-old girl who had recently experienced separation from her parents. They spoke to each other through Kermit the frog (the foster carer) and a penguin puppet (the little girl).

Kermit *Do you live with Auntie Jane and Uncle Jim?*

Penguin *Sometimes.*

Kermit *Where would you like to live?*

Penguin *With my Mummy and Daddy.*

Kermit *Oh, if I could not live with my Mummy and Daddy I would feel very sad.*

Penguin *I feel sad because I cannot live with them.*

Kermit *Why can't you live with your Mummy and Daddy?*

Penguin *Because they are no longer friends and do not love each other.*

Shortly after this conversation, Susan, who had not cried since the separation two weeks before, started to cry because 'permission' to grieve had been given.

Play people

We have used this technique with young children aged three upwards with outstanding success, but we have also used it with older children after having first overcome our own inhibitions. As we said earlier, you need to be able to relax to join in this activity!

You can buy a 'family' of play people at a toy shop. The set we use has been made with recognisable expressions, such as happiness, sadness, anger and so on. There are white, black and mixed parentage play people.

Children who are reluctant to talk directly about how they feel are prepared to talk about how the play people 'feel'. The technique involves telling a story which is basically the child's life story as depicted in the life graph, but transferred to the play people. Telling the story for the first time, we usually just talk about concrete facts: 'This is the mummy and she had a baby girl.' Eventually the child is drawn into the play – which may carry through several sessions – and will start to attribute feelings to the play people which mirror his or her inner world.

Children who have been subjected to acts of violence will frequently work out these experiences again. One child hurled the father figure around the room. Another five-year-old, a girl, was confused because her elderly short-term foster carer had cried when she was moved to an adoptive family. Six months later she was still puzzled, but refused to talk about the incident. With the play people we were able to tell her a story about the little girl who had to move from her 'Nan' whom she loved and this 'Nan' cried. She said, 'When I moved from my Nan she cried and I wanted to cry too but I was afraid to.' From this she was helped to understand what had happened and given reassurance that her 'Nan' was safe and well.

The empty chair

Children will accumulate resentment against adults from their past who have either disappointed or rejected them. Occasionally these feelings can be detected, but usually they remain guarded and unresolved. One way to reach out and bring them into the open is the 'empty chair', a Gestalt therapy technique which we found in Claudia Jewett Jarratt's *Adopting the Older Child*.

Place an empty chair in the centre of the room. Ask the child to imagine that a person with whom he or she has some unfinished business is seated on it. The empty chair helps the child to focus on anything that is left unfinished.

Using dolls can help start a dialogue.

David was interested and curious when we presented him with the empty chair. But he claimed he was unable to think of a suitable occupant for it. 'How about your mother?' we prompted. David then walked purposefully up to the chair and demanded to know, 'Why did you leave me? I want to kick your head in.' With a nervous laugh, he half-heartedly attempted to retract the statement. 'Are you angry with your mother?' we asked. 'Yes I am,' he replied.

It is often possible to use such expressions of anger constructively by encouraging the child to take over the role of the person in the chair so as to experience how the other person feels.

David sat in the chair and imagined he was his Mother, while we pretended to be David. 'Why did you leave me?' I asked. 'I left you because I was quarrelling with your dad and we couldn't live together any more,' came his reply.

The telephone

A toy telephone can be used in a similar way to an empty chair. Your child can be encouraged to 'telephone' a person from the past and have an imaginary conversation with that person. Frequently this is too direct, but can be made less threatening by holding a telephone conversation between either puppets or dolls.

Sarah had been removed from her birth family as a four year old because she had suffered persistent cruelty from her mother's partner. She had been placed in a foster home, but this had broken down after six months. Four months after this breakdown, the following play with dolls and a telephone took place. We made two sets of parents with dolls; the father in one set had an angry face. The dolls were not given names and were not identified as foster parents or birth parents.*

Me *Look at this little girl* (doll). *She cannot live with her birth Mummy. Do you think she will ever take love and care from this forever Mummy and Daddy?*

Sarah *No, she can only take love and care from her birth Mummy and that man who lives with her is no good.*

Me (Gently) *I do not think he is.*

Sarah *Well, he is.* (Sarah then picked up the angry male doll and moved him away from the Mummy doll.)

Me *Look what happens.* (I took the Mummy doll to the angry male doll and reunited them.)

Sarah *But he had gone away.* (She picked up the angry male doll and threw it across the room.)

Me *Now look what happens. The birth Mummy goes and gets him back.*

*This study first appeared in an article in Community Care in December 1982.

A child can be encouraged to 'telephone' a person from the past and have an imaginary conversation with them.

We enacted this several times with Sarah hurling the angry male doll away and me taking the Mummy doll to collect it. Sarah was getting exasperated and announced she was going to 'telephone that Mummy'. She was already familiar with the telephone because we had 'played' with it in the past.

Me *What do they call the Mummy?*

Sarah *Margaret* (the name of her birth mother) *Hello. I want to know why that little girl cannot live with you. Why don't you get rid of the man so this little girl can come and get love and care?*

(At this point Sarah held the telephone out, a look of consternation and disbelief on her face.)

Me *What is the matter?*

Sarah *She has put the phone down on me.*

A powerful urge to pick Sarah up and comfort her hurt almost overwhelmed me. With some effort of will I concentrated on the doll play.

Me *Poor little girl, she is in such a whirl.* (I spun the little girl doll around.) *She doesn't know where to go. She can't get love from her birth Mummy and will not take from the forever Mummy and Daddy.*

Sarah *Yes, she is all empty inside.*

Sarah decided to telephone the little girl and advise her to go and live with the forever Mummy and Daddy because she could get love and care from them. I suggested to Sarah that we should tell her we understand why she wants to love her birth Mummy too.

Sarah *Yes, I know. She can love her birth Mummy, but she cannot live with her because her Mummy does not want this man to go.*

Shortly after this Sarah moved in and eventually settled with a new family.

At no time was this play interpreted to Sarah. For instance, obviously we felt she was the little girl doll, but we never attempted to make this link for her. Violet Oaklander, in *Windows to our Children*, considers that the process of work with the child is a gentle, flowing one, 'an organic event'. The work for Sarah using the dolls and telephone helped her to understand events in her life and start the process of coming to terms with them in a way that was non-threatening. We feel that if we had faced her with direct questions about why her foster placement disrupted, nothing would have been forthcoming.

Role play

With older children, particulary adolescents, one can be more direct. We frequently role play situations by suggesting to the teenagers that we will be them and they be another actor in the scene. This means that they have to 'direct' and be the 'scriptwriter' too. This can be a revealing experience for all concerned.

We discuss role play further in the section about working with adolescents in groups in Chapter 11.

10

Working with black children

All children need a sense of their cultural background.

For help and ideas with this section we are grateful to Beulah Mills, a specialist worker with Leeds Social Services and Janis Blackburn, an ethnic minorities fostering officer in Sheffield, whose contribution originally appeared in Making Life Story Books. We also thank Rose Dagoo, a black social worker/ counsellor, currently working with the Post-Adoption Centre, for her useful comments and additions.

When you are talking to children about their family history, background and future, you will come across many misconceptions they have about themselves. You will find many opportunities to give them a more positive self-image as well as more information about themselves. For Asian, African and Caribbean children and children of mixed parentage there is an extra dimension to their feelings about themselves – colour. Preparation for life story work always needs to be handled with extreme care and honesty, especially when you are trying to put things into their true perspective, and possibly even more so when you are working with black children and black children of mixed-parentage – particularly if you are white.

At the start, if you are white and are doing life story work with such a child, you should be familiar with the correct terminology to use when referring to black people, as incorrect usage of words may inhibit rather than help. Terms such as 'coloured' or 'half-caste' are offensive and should not be used. They deny the child's blackness and the fact that society perceives him or her as black.

If you are white you should recognise that for the child, talking to a white person about race and racism is a poor substitute for talking to a black person. You should therefore make every effort to involve a black worker. Through this helper, many questions can be answered at first hand and a link will be provided with a person with whom the child may be able to identify. This can be particularly useful for children who have been looked after for a great part of their lives and may have had little contact with black people, or for children who are living far removed from their culture.

In many areas, black children who are separated from their birth families are in a tiny minority and white people are the dominant group. For self-protection, or because they have few other models, these children identify with being white and tolerate racist jokes for obvious reasons. Black children who 'think' they are white or try to make themselves white (by scrubbing their skins, for example) are set for a very destructive phase in the future. As with all our children, we need to help them attain a positive self-image and to give them a sense of self-esteem. We need to help them to realise that it is not their being black or of mixed parentage which is the problem, but other people's attitudes to it. However, we also need to keep this matter in perspective and recognise that it is only one of the areas of potential difficulty for them, and that other areas in their lives also need to be given importance.

White workers should try to work through and resolve their own fears and doubts and not underplay issues of race, racism and colour. Otherwise, any discomfort or inhibition will communicate itself to the child who will instinctively sense these barriers. This can lead to communication becoming strained and the child feeling unsafe and unable to trust the worker.

What can you do?

Issues about race, racism and colour are highly complex and charged with feelings, so much so that workers – both black and white – may need a consultant to talk through issues of race and ethnicity, to help put their feelings in perspective. This can help free the workers to clearly define areas that are problematic for them as distinct from those that are problematic for the child.

It is important to a child that the worker doing life story work has a good grasp of the child's world, both the inner world and external realities. This means the worker must familiarise him or herself with aspects of black family life in the context of this society. This involves getting information from a variety of sources, for example, people from a culture similar to that of the child, agencies such as the Commission for Racial Equality (CRE) and the Race Equality Unit at the National Institute for Social Work (NISW), current literature by authors from the child's ethnic background, embassies, etc.

Black people are generally perceived as a homogeneous group and this leads to vast differences in patterns of family life and child rearing being overlooked by professionals. There are enormous cultural, race and class differences in family lifestyles among people from, for example, Guyana; these differences need to be understood and their importance acknowledged.

A child needs to feel valued by the worker and this feeling transmits itself to the child who very soon will get a sense of an adult who knows, 'what it feels like when there aren't any words to say it'. Learning about the child's world demonstrates in a concrete way the value the worker puts on the child.

It is important to remember that a child's life story

does not stop with the move to the new family. In birth families, children are regularly reminded of characteristics they have inherited from relatives and given news of family members and other important people in their lives. This continuity should also be provided for children growing up in substitute families.

Whatever your colour, if you are working with a black or mixed parentage child doing life story work, you need to recognise the ongoing need of that child to talk about race and colour when he or she wishes to. When talking about family life, give children pictures of both black and white families. Ask them to talk about the people in the pictures and ask which are like them. Use this as a starting point for discussion. Ask the child to draw a picture of him or herself as they would like to look. If they present a picture other than of how they are, use this for discussion of different racial looks, talking about characteristics of black and

We went to the Carnival

white people and stressing individual worth above race, whether black or white.

All children need a sense of their cultural background as well as of their family background. Try to get hold of pictures, posters and books of the child's (or their family's) country of origin (see *Further Reading* for titles of some useful books). (Do the same for white children from other countries.) Include pictures of famous black people, especially British black people – writers, politicians, musicians and sportsmen and women – in the collection of material. Stress the achievements of the child's community when the opportunity arises. You might read and let the child have copies of *The Voice, Caribbean Times* or *Asian Times*, for example. Visit or write to black information centres and youth clubs to see what help they can give you. Children may want to know about subjects such as Islam or Rastafarianism, about what kind of food their birth families would eat and about how they should look after their hair and skin. Help them to find out about all these things. If there are festivals in your area, such as a Caribbean carnival, take the child to them. In London, the Commonwealth Institute with its exhibits from all the countries of the Commonwealth is another resource.

Jane's story

Jane is of mixed parentage, with a father of Caribbean origin and a white British mother. Her mother had had an unhappy home life and left home at an early age to go to Liverpool. There she met Jane's father. They had a happy relationship and their first baby, Jane's sister, was welcome and well cared for. The relationship began to break up and when she found she was pregnant again, Jane's mother was unhappy. By the time Jane was born her father had all but disappeared and Jane's birth was an unwelcome event.

By the time she was four Jane was in care; her older sister stayed with their mother. An attempt was made to place Jane in a long-term foster home, but this did not work out. Her mother was still concerned about her, but did not feel that Jane could ever return to her. When Jane was eight years old, it was decided that a second attempt should be made to foster her. This time a life story book was made before the placement.

During the process of making the book, it became clear that Jane did not really believe that she had a father or that she was of mixed parentage.

Jane had said that she was not prepared to leave the children's home and she would go and hide if her social worker came to talk to her about fostering. She agreed, however, to make a life story book because she wanted to know more about herself. By drawing her family tree, talking about her birth certificate and discussing the 'facts of life', Jane came to accept that she had a father and that he had a name and could be talked about.

The next stage was to get Jane to accept that her father was black and that she therefore had a place in the black community as well as the white one. I offered to get maps, photographs and posters of the island where her father came from. Jane eventually accepted this offer and started to talk to the other children and staff about her father. She faced derision from the other children but she was so fascinated by discovering her 'other half' that it did not deter her.

Being of mixed parentage had bothered Jane for a long time, but she had never found an opportunity to talk about it. Now that she could talk about it with more confidence, she could easily identify where her father had come from and she could see from her birth certificate who both her parents were. Because of her concern for Jane, her mother had willingly given photographs of her before she came into care, although she had no photograph of Jane's father.

By the time the life story book was up to date and Jane had also been given the opportunity to discuss the breakdown of her previous fostering, she felt secure enough in her sense of identity to consider trying again. She was placed with a new family and felt happy talking to them about her birth parents, and saw this was accepted by them when she showed them her life story book. She was adopted by this new family a year later.

Jane needed knowledge about all her past, part of which was that she was of mixed parentage. It was an important part of all the things she needed to sort out.

11

Working with groups

Working with families

When there is more than one looked after child in a family, it is possible to do some of the work of making a life story book together but it is important that each child has his or her own record of their life story work. We have found that working with a family in a group progresses faster than working in a one-to-one situation. The work will, of course, depend on the ages of the children in the family. With older children you might consider using a modified form of the group programme for adolescents, described in the next section.

Normally it will be the oldest child who will provide the link for the others from past to present. That child may be the family 'historian', assisting you in helping the other members of the family to understand what has happened in their past and what is happening in the present. In doing so, the older children are able to extend their own knowledge and understanding too, and can begin to explain to their siblings how they understand things. This can be less threatening than explaining to someone outside the family.

In working with sibling groups, again it is important to bear in mind the issue of undisclosed sexual abuse. It may be that only one child in a sibling group has disclosed, but that group discussion prompts other siblings to disclose. It is also important to remember that older siblings are more likely to have been pressured into silence themselves and could deny that abuse has taken place when younger members of the family disclose that they have been abused. In these situations it may be more useful to do individual sessions with each of the siblings before doing work as a family group.

With a sibling group, we might ask how the oldest child can explain to the other siblings why they became separated from their family of origin. Marie, 14 years old and the eldest of four children, felt that she had been the cause because of her 'bad behaviour'. When she declared this, it was a revelation to her to find out that a younger brother and sister felt they were the cause too. From there, they were helped to reach an understanding of their mother's mental illness. They understood that there were reasons why they were now living in a children's home and that there was no need to seek to blame anyone, or take the blame upon themselves, because the causes were beyond their control.

Working with adolescents in groups

We have shown how working with children from the same family can help in the process of life story work. Working with a group of children who are not related can also be successful.

Children over twelve who have been looked after for many years become unwilling to talk about their past, confused about the present and have little sense of hope for the future. We have found that providing a setting in which children share their pasts, their feelings about the present and their hopes for the future with others who have experienced similar difficulties can be a help and a comfort. A group preparation can be a way of reducing the sense of isolation many children feel and a means of freeing them to share similar feelings with others.

Children who are looked after often consider that their families are abnormal and it can be a revelation to them that their families are like many others. One group of five children discovered in their exploration that not only had none of them ever met their fathers, or had not done so for many years, but also that they all came from many-fathered families and all had half-brothers and sisters. No amount of assurance from an adult could, we feel, have helped these children to place their families in context as 'normal' as much as talking and sharing with their peers had.

To help get over the natural reluctance to discuss the past, present and future, we have worked out a programme of meetings (eight core meetings and then a few follow-up meetings) which divide roughly into three stages. The first stage is to help the young people to develop an awareness of themselves, to begin to express their inner thoughts and feelings, and to look at the range of options open to a looked after child – of which fostering is but one. How making a life story book might help is introduced as a discussion topic about half-way through this stage and books are made individually during the second stage.

'Bridging' work (see page 35), the third stage, which is done partially within the group, can start only when the possibility of return to the birth family or a move to a foster family is imminent. Sometimes we have enlisted the help of children who have made life story books and who have been successfully placed during this bridging stage. This greatly facilitates discussion about hopes and fears, as well as injecting an element of reality.

Forming and working with a group

The group should be carefully selected. It is a working group which can perhaps accommodate one disruptive member, but rarely more. All the children's foster carers or social workers or residential social workers must have agreed in advance that they do life story work with their child and understand what they will be taking on in doing this. Meetings can be arranged with those involved with the child to explain the broad outline of what you are doing and to discuss the

problems of possible regression.

Usually we work with six children and two to three leaders. The initial groupwork runs for eight weekly sessions of about one and a half hours and includes the sharing of a simple meal. Planning and recording takes a further two hour meeting of the leaders each week. At session three the idea of a life story book is introduced.

The aim of such a group is to provide an atmosphere in which the children can talk freely about their doubts and fears. Of course the comments we have made earlier about confidentiality apply here too. Our major source of ideas about the content of such groups comes from Violet Oaklander's *Windows to our Children* and we suggest that you read this book as part of your preparation. We describe here the content of the group sessions, which, as with other ideas in this book, you may need to adapt to your own needs.

Depending on the time of year, and the time available, we have found it valuable to arrange a trip out early in the life of the group and additional to the normal sessions. This, we find, helps to form a group identity.

A programme for group work
Session one

Before this first meeting each child will have been visited by one of the leaders and been given a personal explanation of what will be happening.

The session starts with a brief explanation of the aims and purposes of the group and an introduction of the group members. Then we start work with some 'warm up' exercises in which everyone is involved. For example, we sit in a circle and throw a ball between us, first calling out our own name and then throwing a ball to a group member and calling out their name, until the ball has passed to each person.

We use the game 'I went to market and bought some apples'. The next person repeats this and adds a word beginning with the next letter of the alphabet. They might say, 'I went to market and bought some apples and bananas.' The next person might say, 'I went to market and bought some apples, some bananas and some cauliflowers,' and so on through the alphabet.

We then move on to 'brainstorming' ideas. For this we have a flip chart mounted on an easel. The children call out ideas related to the topic under consideration and these are written down on the flip chart. If any child is prepared to do the writing we let them do so. Two or three topics can be covered in a session. The first brainstorm topic is 'Why are we here?' We use the contributions on the flip chart as a basis for discussion and soon we break for a simple meal, during which the discussion continues.

We then have a brainstorming session to create 'Feelings' cards like those discussed on page 24. The purpose of this activity is to introduce the concept of words to describe emotions. Ask the children to call out words that describe feelings, like sad, happy, angry and so on. Write these down on individual cards. Then the group, including the leaders, draw faces to match the feelings. Continue this game with individuals miming a 'feeling'.

The final brainstorming session is on 'What is a family?' The ideas of what constitutes a family are then used in the discussion. Remember at this stage not to force the pace of the group or try and lead it where it does not want to go.

Finish the session with some group game, perhaps a repetition of 'I went to market'.

Session two

Open the session with the group's very own game, 'I went to market'. The group has to try and recall the correct sequence from the previous week. Return to the work on 'feelings' cards with further miming of the faces, and then asking the group to identify feelings that can be attributed to a face. Write these

'feelings' down on the cards.

The simple meal could take place at this point or after the first brainstorming session, as appropriate.

The brainstorm topic is 'Why do children come to be 'looked after'?' This could be threatening to members of the group and you may prefer to distance it for them by drawing either a boy or a girl on the flip chart, give it a name and entitle the session 'Why did Andrew (or Jade) come to be looked after?' Use the material for discussion, gently moving the discussion towards how 'Andrew' might have felt. Encourage the use of the 'feelings' words introduced earlier.

What Violet Oaklander calls a 'fantasy trip' could follow. She suggests that relaxation exercises are useful before starting the work itself. We use several, for example:

Close your eyes. Starting with your toes, tense them. Gradually move up your body, tensing each muscle. Foot, leg, thigh and so on, right up to the head. Now let out all that tension slowly, feel it ebb away.

Then ask the group to close their eyes and take them on a fantasy trip. (This will lead to a drawing session, so have a supply of paper and colouring pencils ready.)

Let's pretend we're on an island. Take a walk through the island. Notice things: the colours of the flowers, the birds, the animals, fruit on the trees, the noises and smells. Suddenly, you enter a clearing and there is a big castle. Enter the courtyard. Walk across it. Enter the big hall. It is empty. You notice a staircase. Climb the stairs. At the top of the staircase there is a long corridor. You walk along it and you notice there are names on the doors. At the door with your name on it you stop. Enter the room. Have a good look round. Notice things. How does the room look? One last look around. Right, now open your eyes.

Now ask the group not to speak, but to draw a picture of what they saw in the room. The leaders can draw pictures too.

When the pictures are ready, a leader asks individuals to share their drawings with them. Let the children describe the picture in their own words. Do not be tempted to interpret the picture back. Instead, for example, if a child has drawn a settee, you might ask what the settee is either thinking or feeling. What is it saying? We usually write down the child's comments on the drawing, encouraging the use of 'feeling' words where this is appropriate.

Violet Oaklander believes that it is important to encourage children to share themselves. She regards it as a means of 'promoting the child's self discovery by asking him to elaborate on the parts of the picture. Making parts clearer, more obvious. Describing the shapes, forms, colours, representations, objects and people.'

You could finish off this session by playing a quiet game like 'sleeping lions'. Everyone stretches out on the floor and pretends to be a sleeping lion. One member, without physically touching anyone, attempts to get the others to move. He or she can pull faces, pretend to jump on a group member, blow on them, but must not touch anyone. Any movement or noise means that a person is no longer a sleeping lion and is therefore out of the game.

Session three

Start with a group game, perhaps 'I went to market' once again. Have a brainstorming session on 'What is a children's home?' and follow this up with discussion. Go on to a brainstorming session on 'How did Andrew feel on his first day being looked after?' and follow this with role playing about 'Andrew' being looked after with the children playing different roles.

The meal break might follow this, with the discussion continuing.

Another of Violet Oaklander's fantasy trips could then be introduced.

Close your eyes. Imagine you are a rose. What kind of rose bush are you? Are you very small? Are you large? Are you fat? Are you tall? Do you have flowers? If so, what kind? What are your stems and branches like? What are your roots like? Do you have any roots? Do you have leaves? What kind? Do you have thorns? Where are you? In a yard? In a park? In the desert? In the city? In the country? In the middle of the ocean?

Are you in a pot, or growing in the ground, or through cement, or even inside somewhere? What's around you? Are there flowers or are you alone? Are there trees, animals, people, birds?

Do you look like a rose bush or something else? Is there anything around you, like a fence; if so, what is it like? Or are you just in an open place?

What's it like to be a rose bush? How do you survive? Does someone take care of you?

What's the weather like for you right now?

Open your eyes. Draw yourself as a rosebush. *

Encourage the children to tell you about their drawings individually. Write on the drawing the thoughts and feelings of the rose bush. Do not be tempted to interpret the picture to the child.

Now is the time to introduce the idea of the life story book. First, brainstorm the question: What are life story books? One group's contributions to the flipchart were:

You read them	I don't like them
Birds and the bees	You put photographs in them
Biography	
	Horrid
You write them	
	Feel bad if you don't talk
You enjoy them	about things

*This passage is extracted from Violet Oaklander's Windows to our Children.

Use the material on the flipchart for discussion, acknowledging and accepting that making a life story book can be painful. Lead into how someone will be offering to make a life story book with each one of them. Finish this session with a quiet game.

Following this session, you should have a meeting with those who will be working individually on making a life story book with each child. The purpose is to share the broad outline of the group work, to explain how you have been using the material, and for mutual support. This meeting is particularly important if the child is displaying signs of regression.

Session four

Open with a simple game. The work can be more loosely structured from now on. Sometimes we bring in a box of 'play people' and glove puppets and wait for the children to take the lead. Frequently we have conversations between the dolls and puppets, talking about what they are thinking and feeling. This may lead to role playing from something either a doll or a puppet has been 'saying'.

For another group activity a leader has a large sheet of card on which he or she draws a shape, then might say and write, 'This is me, in a red circle. I am all alone.' Someone else then draws a shape anywhere on the card, makes a comment and writes it down. (If we know that one of the group has difficulty with writing, one of the leaders takes responsibility for writing down all the comments.) The game continues until everyone has drawn at least two shapes.

Fit into the flow of the work any of these brainstorms: What is a family? What is a children's home? What is a foster family? It is sometimes useful to return to earlier brainstorm topics such as what is a children's home. The group's perceptions will change with time.

Allow the children to express their feelings. If they make negative comments, do not try to persuade them differently. These topics usually raise fears about confidentiality. If so, reassure the group. You might lead on from this to a brainstorm on 'Who can you trust?'

If there is time during the session, we use Vera Fahlberg's three parents model (see page 38) to discuss how being looked after changes birth parents' rights and responsibilities, to reassure the children that no one is trying to take away what they were endowed with at birth and to explain the position of the foster carers.

Session five

Open with 'I went to market' followed by a group game, such as 'You've done it again, Mabel'. In this game, players stand in a circle with one member in the centre. Another player jumps into the circle and says, 'You've done it again, Mabel, you've (for example) not paid the rent for five weeks.' The first person can either respond to this by explaining why 'Mabel has done it again' or admit that this is so by rejoining the circle. If 'Mabel' goes out, the accuser becomes the new 'Mabel' and another player jumps into the circle adding another accusation, 'You've done it again Mabel, you've...' and so the game continues, until everyone has had a turn or interest begins to wane. The group then breaks for its simple meal together.

Afterwards we use a poem recommended by Violet Oaklander.* It was written by an eight-year-old Turkish girl and translated. Read it aloud while the group sits, eyes closed. (This poem can produce a powerful reaction, so you will have to try and gauge whether the group is ready for it.)

The group then draws pictures and the leaders talk to each child about their picture.

*Reproduced from Have you Seen a Comet?: Children's art and writing from around the world (U.S. Committee for Unicef, New York and the John Day Company.)

THERE IS A KNOT INSIDE ME

There is a knot inside me
A knot which cannot be untied
Strong
It hurts
As if they had put a stone
Inside of me
I always remember the old days
Playing at our summer house
Going to grandmother's
Staying at grandmother's
I want those days to return
Perhaps the knot will be untied when they return.
But there is a knot inside of me
So strong
It hurts
As if it is a stone inside of me.

One 13-year-old girl wrote her own poem which we use too*.

I'd like to fly
I'd like to but I can't
I wasn't meant to
but I want to
I was meant to be me.

Why?
For some reason!
I wish I was a bird
to fly and be free
I feel I am imprisoned

In anyway I am what
I am nobody can change
that or make that
but I wish.

You could suggest that they draw Andrew/Jade from session three with their knot inside them. This could lead to discussion of how Andrew/Jade might tell the others in the children's home how they feel inside.

By this stage in the life of the group you need to be sensitive to the issues the group might want to raise. For example, group members, especially if they are older children, might have experienced foster care breakdowns and may want to talk about this.

* Reproduced by kind permission of Angie

One group brainstormed the advantages and disadvantages of being in a foster home:

Advantages	Disadvantages
Somewhere to go and live	Break down
Improves your life	Ruins your life
You like them	Waste of time
Better than your own home	Isn't your own home

At the end of the session close with a quiet, relaxing game.

Session six

Open with a game. It could be a 'scribble game' (from Violet Oaklander). Everyone stands with space around them. They close their eyes and pretend to scribble on a giant sheet of paper. Then they are each given paper and pens and close their eyes and reproduce this scribble on their paper. When they open their eyes they try to identify the shapes produced.

From here they can go on to draw a picture of a time when they were laughed at. If this is too threatening, they can draw a time when Jade/Andrew was laughed at. Alternatively they can take another fantasy trip in which a boat in a storm is described while the group sits, eyes closed. Then the group draws what they saw. The simple meal can be taken together after this.

Move on to a group story. We have some cards with pictures of houses, cars, a cat, a dog, an eagle, items of clothing and so on. We put a picture on the table and say something about it, for example. 'This is a house in a town.' The next person says something further about it, such as 'and the stick of dynamite came along to blow it up.' In one group someone put down a picture of a cat and added, 'Along came a lion and started to roar.' This was ridiculed by the group and used to discuss when we pretend about things.

You could then go on to brainstorm 'How can we find foster families?'

In dealing with this subject with older children we try and help them understand how difficult it is to find substitute families for them. This can be discussed before the brainstorming session and it can be followed with a discussion about how to recruit substitute or foster families.

By this stage the children will be meeting their individual social workers and be working on life story books. We look at what they are doing and the ways that it might be of help in placement.

We might use role playing here:

Foster carers being interviewed

Andrew/Jade's first visit to a new foster family

A problem which might arise in a foster family, like Andrew being caught smoking or Jade being accused of stealing

We stop the role play frequently in mid-stream and get the participants to change roles. We encourage them to talk about how it 'felt' in the role. We stop the role play and invite the group to say what a child's or foster carer's or social worker's secret voice might be saying inside them. If appropriate we use the candle technique (see page 36) to complement 'three parents' from the earlier session.

We close as usual with a relaxing game.

Session seven

We use this session to illustrate how a life story book can be helpful by enlisting the help of an older child who has made one and has been in placement for some time. This child needs to feel secure and you will have to spend time with him or her assisting with the preparation. Towards the end of the session the child's foster carers might be included in the discussion as well. If children have experienced a foster care disruption, they often interrupt the session to talk about their experiences and make comparisons.

Thomas, whose story we told earlier on page 34, has spoken to groups about his life. When he reached the part of his story where he met his birth mother for the first time, it produced a barrage of questions: 'What was it like?' 'Did you cry?' 'Did she cry?' 'Did you kiss each other?' Thomas's reply stunned them. 'No, I didn't feel anything. It could have been someone in the street. I felt nothing.'

One child asked Thomas how he had expected his mother to be. 'Tall and rich' was the wry reply. This, of course, vividly demonstrated how we all have fantasy pictures in our minds.

Frequently the group will use this session to talk about their feelings about their birth families. The group should close on a note of optimism as they understand how making a life story book to establish the past is helpful.

Session eight

This is the final session of the first phase and needs to be organised around the feelings of loss that will be felt by all. Open by talking about the previous session. Ask members to draw something they remember from it and use their drawings for discussion.

Have the simple meal together, with perhaps a special treat to mark the occasion. Go on to brainstorm 'What was this group about? What should be included in the next group for other children?' Follow with a quiet drawing session in which the members of the group might draw cards for each other. End with a brainstorm on 'How do we feel?'

There should be at least two follow-up group meetings at six-weekly intervals. Before they go, remind the group of this and that they will be meeting together again.

Before the next meeting get together with the children's individual workers to talk about the progress they are making with the life story work and to discuss the broad features of the group.

Session nine

This should be arranged about six weeks after the core group finishes. If substitute families have been found for some of the children, the focus can be orientated towards 'bridging' work. Whenever possible the leaders should have made contact at least once during the intervening six weeks. Send a letter about a week before the meeting to remind the child of the date, and suggest in it that they might like to bring along their life story book.

The session can be loosely structured around what you have done in earlier sessions. We find that many children are prepared to share their life story books with the group. This can lead to a discussion of the feelings invoked while making the books.

Inevitably expectations will have been aroused about substitute families. With older children these may not be fulfilled. The group will need to look at the reality of this and be helped to talk about their disappointment and frustrations.

During the six-week interval before the next meeting, there will be further meetings with the children's individual social workers.

Session ten

The purpose of this session is to reinforce the skills acquired through the group meetings: the ability of the children to talk about their hopes, fears and pain. The focus of this meeting will depend upon what has happened or is about to happen in their lives. If some children are now in placement, sharing their experiences might be usefully explored. We have used material from *Challenge of Fostering** to give children some insight into how moving into a foster family can affect them. We have concentrated on that part of the material which confronts foster carers with the changes they will have to make. Frequently children have not considered the fact that foster carers have to make adjustments too.

Ideally there should be further meetings at intervals as a means of helping the group members to give mutual support to one another. Between these meetings there should be further discussion with the children's individual foster carers.

Challenge of Fostering is a basic training course for foster carers designed by the National Foster Care Association.

12

Working with children with a learning disability Ann Atwell

Children with a learning disability have the same 'child' needs as any other child, and this means having an accurate account of their personal history.

There can be a reluctance to become involved in life story work with children who have a learning disability, and those involved with these children need to examine their own feelings about this. One of the most common reasons is that some social workers are themselves quite uncomfortable with learning disabilities and may as a result avoid contact. It is important to recognise this and either accept it and not become involved in work with people with learning disabilities or undertake additional training to help overcome any difficulty. A second problem with undertaking this work is where the worker has difficulty in communicating with a disabled person, and is unable or unwilling to take time to learn how the disabled person most readily communicates. Thirdly, there is sometimes a wish to be overprotective of the child with learning disabilities, thus avoiding any work which has the potential to be upsetting or painful.

Another barrier to life story work is the continuing belief that families who would wish to take on a child with learning disabilities will not be found. This can lead to deferment of vital work until a family has been identified, which does not allow the disabled child space and time to internalise their own life history and grieve the loss of their birth family before moving to a new family.

How communication happens

One of the most common reasons for life story work not being undertaken is the belief that the young person's learning disabilities are too severe, therefore the work is pointless. But take the case of Fiona, aged 13. She had severe learning disabilities as well as being physically disabled. She was the size of a three year old and spent most of her time stripped naked in her cot, having divested herself of all her clothing and bedding except for one cover under which she hid, sitting in the corner of her cot in the foetal position. She had only a few tufts of hair due to pulling it out in handfuls, her skin was bleeding and scarred from self abuse through picking and biting it, she had frequent screaming tantrums and banged her head regularly. She could not walk or talk, and she resisted overtures by staff to get close and cuddle her. Because it was unclear how much she understood, the only life story work done was to talk to her regularly about where her family was and why she was in hospital, as well as about the plan to move her to a foster family. This produced no response from Fiona except her usual tantrums.

Once in placement, Fiona showed some ability to understand the world and to convey her wishes. For example, whenever the family went on a car trip to the nearby town where Fiona used to live, she recognised the town from the outskirts and became agitated and distressed. This happened on every occasion so could not be dismissed as coincidence. She also frequently had a tantrum as they were setting off on a car journey, but eventually settled down. Through time the foster father wondered whether Fiona's 'tantrum' was Fiona's way of reminding him to fasten his seat belt, which he normally didn't do until round the first corner from their house (about 30 yards). When this theory was tested out it proved to be the case. When the foster father 'belted up' Fiona didn't have her usual tantrum. Both of these situations had previously been attributed to 'Fiona just having one of her tantrums' and only through keen observation was it realised that she was communicating. So one of the fundamental lessons of Fiona's story is not to assume that those with severe learning disabilities cannot communicate, but to question our own ability to understand how the communication is being made.

Where to begin is often seen as a problem, but understanding the child is fundamental and will dictate where and how to begin. For example, if a child is hyperactive and has poor concentration, it is perhaps pointless to consider traditional life story work, since the method of sitting and writing and drawing will be particularly difficult for a hyperactive child. John was such a child and instead of making a book, he made more sense of frequent repetitive tours round the area where he grew up, with visits to the family home and local shops, parks, etc, all of which were captured on video film. Even though John rarely watched television normally, he was captivated by seeing himself on TV along with people and places recognisable to him, and he would watch this over and over again, telling anyone who cared to listen where and what the pictures were. Such a combination of methods which includes physically visiting people and places of significance and recording them on video combined to produce an understandable and readily accessible life story for John.

Who should do life story work?

In deciding how to tackle life story work with children with learning disabilities, it is also important to consider who would be best able to do this work. Since being able to understand and communicate with the child is paramount, this should be undertaken by the person who communicates best with the child, rather than assume it is always done by the child's social worker. For example, a worker in a residential home may be the most significant as well as most trusted adult for the child. For some children who may previously have spent a considerable time at home there will be a wealth of family knowledge still contained in the family which will be vital for the child's life story work. For example, they may be able to identify things from family life to include in a life story video or book. Sometimes there is a toy or family ornament which has a story attached to it or was a particular favourite, or sometimes a piece of music like a theme tune for a TV programme may have particular family significance. By incorporating such stimuli it is easier to sustain the attention of the young person and help make connections.

Using different methods

For children with a learning disability who perhaps have difficulty in communicating by speech, or who may lack the use of one or more of the senses, it is possible to develop life story work which does not depend only on visual methods but involves stimulation of other senses. For example, for David who was blind, much of his life story work was interspersed with tactile stimuli, for example, buttons from a favourite person's jacket, a shell from a seaside outing with the family, dried flowers from the garden. It also included a handkerchief perfumed with the birth mother's favourite perfume. For a child such as David it is also more helpful to use audio rather than visual methods of life story work, and his written life story was also recorded on audio tape. It is possible to convey a spoken message from the birth parent by this method, rather than the more traditional letter which some parents write to their child. This naturally would depend on how appropriate it was at that point to involve the parent to this degree. Positive involvement of the birth parent in this way, as in video life stories, is possible. What greater stimulus could there be for a child than to hear the voice or see the face of their parent or another family member. Such work assumes co-operation by the birth family. Where the family has been through the painful process of relinquishing the child, it is often a helpful way of them being constructively involved in part of the child's future.

In contemplating life story work for a child who has a severe learning disability and who may have lived in an institutional setting for some years, one of the difficulties can be that the child has no understanding, or at best a very poor understanding, of 'normal family life'. Before helping such a child plan for a move to substitute family care, for example, it is necessary to find a method of life story work which helps the child understand the notion of 'family' in the first place. Stuart was such a boy, and by means of a cardboard pop-up house and cut-out people shapes, on to which were pasted the real photographic faces of family members and staff and children at the children's home, some work was done to give Stuart a sense of who belonged in which household. Since Stuart's mother and brother were going to be significant people for him, and regular contact would continue in his new family placement, a further pop-up home was made to represent the new family. Their cut-outs were added to their pop-up house. It was then possible to work over some sessions with Stuart to convey that his birth mother and brother would spend time in the new house, as well as conveying to Stuart that he would move from the children's home to the new house and new family.

Some caution might be needed in adopting a 'third object' approach to life story work, since this can sometimes complicate the task or confuse the child with learning disabilities who might not readily make a connection between, say, a puppet and him or herself, or a story about an animal. Far better to work with direct references and keep this as simple as possible and appropriate to that particular child's skills and abilities.

Even for a child who has only a mild to moderate learning disability, and who therefore may have writing and drawing skills, the traditional life story book may not necessarily be the preferred way to record the child's history. For example, if a child has writing and drawing skills but is not interested in sitting down to this sort of work and would rather be playing with computer games, it may be possible to engage the help of someone with computer skills who can computerise the child's history in a way that stimulates the child's interest.

In summary:

Don't be afraid to tackle this work.

Decide who is the best person to do the work.

Understand the means of communication.

Identify the child's skills and interests.

Construct a method or methods that take account of this.

You can develop life story work which does not depend on visual methods but involves the stimulation of other senses.

13

Working with children who have been sexually abused Gerrilyn Smith

To do life story work with children who have been sexually abused you will need to adapt some of the skills and tasks already described in previous chapters. The sexual abuse of some of the children you will work with will be known about and may have resulted in their being removed from their families of origin. Work with these children is less problematic than with those children where sexual abuse in their family of origin has not been disclosed.

Children known to have been sexually abused

It is important if you are working with a child where it is known that they have been sexually abused, that you acknowledge the abuse. This can save a lot of time in doing life story work. Many children in the care system do not know what other people know about them. They may not know if it is alright to talk about their past experiences. By raising the subject of sexual abuse early on, you are signalling to the child that you will talk about it with them. You may also want to know who else has talked about it with the child. If very little work has been done with the child about their experience of abuse, you need to prepare yourself for a longer task than you originally bargained for. Life story work should not replace therapy. The life story work should remain task-centred, recording important past experiences that they can keep. Talking with you now will make talking in therapy easier later on. It may be whilst doing life story work that it becomes clear to you or to the older child with whom you are working that further work needs to be done.

There are some important messages you need to convey to the child about their experience of sexual abuse.

Belief

It is important that you demonstrate your belief that it did happen. You may also want to explore why it is difficult for children to tell about sexual abuse, and to suggest that sometimes, after children have told, they remember other things about the abuse that they haven't told people. You need to let the child know it is okay to remember. You may also want to discuss why some children would prefer to forget or say it didn't happen when it did. You could make a list of people who believed the child and people who did not, including members of the child's family and extended family. This can help a child understand why they are no longer living with their family of origin. If their

original family did not believe sexual abuse had happened, it will be impossible for them to protect the child in the future.

Right and wrong

You need to offer some comments about the rights and wrongs of sexual abuse which are developmentally appropriate, for example: 'It is right for children to tell adults.' 'It is wrong for adults to sexually abuse children.' These may be important messages to give those children who are showing signs of sexual bullying, or who are clearly sexually offending against other children. You may need to show that you understand why a child might sexually offend against other children, but that a history of sexual victimisation is not an excuse to do it to others.

What happened

It may be useful to record from the child's point of view what happened when they told. What did their mum say or do? What about their dad? Their brothers and sisters? It can be helpful to record what the child would have liked to happen. This is important as it not only identifies and records what did happen, but also provides the child with a model response that can inform both their current carers and the child as a future parent.

If the child is looked after and the offender is still in the family, the child may have strong feelings that they are being punished for telling. Be honest about the unfairness of the situation: it is unfair that children are deprived of their family because an adult won't own up to having a serious problem. You may be able to identify whom the child would like to have contact with and what might be safe circumstances under which contact could occur.

Many of the other tasks and suggestions identified in this book can be used with children who have been sexually abused. You need to be prepared for the confusions they will express if no one has talked about the meaning of their abuse with them before.

Children who have been sexually abused can have both positive and negative feelings about the perpetrators. Reinforce whatever feelings they have. If they have no positive feelings that is okay. The same is true for a child who has no negative feelings. Avoid making assumptions about how the child should feel about the perpetrator or other members of their family. It can be useful to recognise and record that that is how they feel right now. This leaves room for the child to change how they feel at a future date.

Some children who have been sexually abused may not be ready to do life story work when you are. This may be because remembering their past abuse is too traumatic for them and makes them feel worse. They could experience flashbacks during the sessions. Workers should therefore go at the pace of the child. If the child is clear they do not feel able to talk about the abuse in more detail at this time you should let them know that is okay. You should help the child understand why acknowledging the sexual abuse is important for the adults who will be caring for him or her in the future. It may be sufficient to record something like "X' was touched in ways she didn't like by her dad. She doesn't feel able to talk about it now but maybe she will in the future.'

You can still make comments indicating your belief, and your position on the moral issues surrounding what happened. You could even speculate about what the child might like to have happened.

If you use euphemisms for sexual abuse, select one that the child has used or feels comfortable with. There is no need for explicit detail about what happened. A life story book can help teach a child the difference between private and public; as a book is for public consumption so the material included needs to reflect the public consumption of private experiences. Many children I see for therapy bring their life story books with them to one of the early sessions as a way of introducing themselves to me.

Undisclosed sexual abuse

If a child has not disclosed sexual abuse but it is suspected, workers may wish to suggest to the child that they or other professionals were worried that the child had been sexually abused. Before doing this the workers need to feel clear that the child is safe (i.e., not currently being abused) and to know what their agency procedures are in the event of a clear

disclosure. If this is likely to require investigation by a primary investigation team, then the worker will need to tell the child what will happen next and why it needs to be followed up. If the child discloses abuse in their family of origin and they currently reside elsewhere, but still have contact with their family of origin, you will need to consider how to manage the future contact. It may be appropriate to consider cancelling it until a more detailed assessment can be made.

If a child discloses abuse in their current placement this will need to be investigated by a primary investigation team. It is important you explain this to the child, as they may need to be moved.

Sometimes a child makes a partial disclosure. He or she may tell about being sexually abused but not identify the perpetrator. You can still carry on with life story work incorporating the issues raised above, perhaps speculating as to why it is hard for the child to identify who sexually abused them.

Conclusion

This is only a brief summary of issues to consider in doing life story work with children who have been sexually abused. Children do disclose new abuse when doing life story work. This may be because it provides the child with space to reflect on their past experiences, or the focus of the task makes it possible for the child to talk about it, in a way that therapy or counselling did not.

If it becomes clear that more work needs to be done or that the life story work is triggering traumatic memories that impede the child's normal development, referral for therapy should perhaps be considered and life story work suspended until the child is more emotionally secure in the present, rather than traumatised by the past and any mention of it. Workers need to be familiar with their agency's policy and procedures and understand where life story work fits in, especially when dealing with new disclosures of information that raise further child protection issues.

14

Life story work in other settings

There are many different circumstances in which life story work can be used to facilitate communication and help children, and adults, through painful periods of their lives. Maureen Hitcham, Jean Lovie and Gerrilyn Smith describe three different contexts in which life story work has proved effective.

Life story work with children suffering a life threatening illness
Maureen Hitcham

The diagnosis of childhood cancer is an unwanted, unexpected and devastating discovery. Although the outlook for most newly diagnosed children is optimistic there can be no guarantees of a cure. The sad reality is that many will suffer some form of emotional disturbance and/or physical disability. Some will bravely struggle with the illness and its treatment but die.

Life story books and video diaries can help such children and their families cope with the intense feelings and emotions aroused when living with the strain and uncertainty of a life threatening condition.

Stephen's Story
I met Stephen on my first day as a Malcolm Sargent social worker. He was a bright, mischievous four-year-old with a lively personality and good sense of humour; he also had cancer. My plans for him included a life story book. One month after we met I drove Stephen to his parents' home with the news that he had only days to live. I had sensed and been on the receiving end of his frustration and anger, much of which was directed at the intravenous drip administering the chemotherapy which made him feel so sick. We managed only two small pieces of work – the first was the planned used of drawings to acknowledge and deal with Stephen's anger. He scribbled fiercely over some of the drawings saying how much he hated the drip.

The second piece of work was my spontaneous response to hearing he had only days to live. It was mid-December and he was going home to celebrate the arrival of Father Christmas early. We spent the last hour before leaving the hospital making a Christmas card for his parents. Despite being very weak and very breathless, Stephen worked enthusiastically and with great excitement. There was a real sense of achievement for both of us on

I don't like you drip
I would like to punch you because you make me feel sick

In this drawing, Stephen compares the facial expressions before and after dealing with his anger

completion. I know now that this was also my way of saying sorry to his parents for all the things I had not been able to do. Stephen died on 18 December at home.

Sadly there isn't always the luxury of time to plan, when working with gravely ill children. This does not mean that we should disregard good practice, but we may have to acknowledge at the outset that many of the agreed goals may not be reached despite a willingness and determination on the part of both child and worker. Workers may subsequently be left with a number of unresolved feelings. In view of the complexity and diversity of the social work task in working with these children, regular professional and managerial supervision is essential.

This is an emotional area of work and it is normal and proper to respond emotionally. The techniques I describe here all evoke strong emotional responses, so self awareness and an understanding of the implications for the child are essential before embarking on this work. There also needs to be an awareness of personal feelings regarding death not only as an abstract notion but more importantly, perhaps, as a personal reality. These techniques can all be adapted to suit you as an individual and the child with whom you are working.

Studies have shown that children who have cancer are more anxious than other children. Many of them keep their thoughts and feelings to themselves for a variety of reasons. It is important that they understand what is happening and why, so that they are able to distinguish reality from fantasy.

Graeme's story

Graeme is seven years old and suffers from Aplastic Anaemia. Although not a malignant disease, its treatment and implications are similar to cancer. As part of his treatment Graeme had to undergo a bone marrow transplant which is a major and hazardous procedure. Patients undergoing transplantation are at risk of infection and therefore are nursed in a sterile environment. All staff and visitors must wear gowns and masks and observe strict rules of hygiene.

The period of isolation, limitations on normal activity, restrictions on diet and free movement inevitably took their toll on Graeme. Not surprisingly he could be surly, aggressive and very demanding. No-one felt sure how Graeme was feeling or what his understanding of the illness and treatment was.

Graeme did not easily share thoughts and feelings and was not well enough or interested enough to undertake traditional life story work. But in his case,

producing a video diary seemed to have provided him with a non-threatening and enjoyable opportunity to sort out and know the facts about his illness and its treatment, which hopefully left him feeling less at the mercy of uncontrollable events.

He was in fact the first child with whom I used a video camera and his response was remarkable. On film, he freely shares his thoughts, feelings and understanding of his condition and its treatment. He describes how there is a war going on inside his body called the SS War: SS meaning Saddam and Smith (his surname). Saddam represents the bad cells, Smith the good cells. He humorously and imaginatively describes the chemotherapy bombing Saddam in order to make room for the good cells to grow. When asked who he thought would win the war he replied, 'Well, at first I thought it would be Saddam but now I think it will be Smith!' Graeme proudly showed his family and staff this short video and later went on to record further footage discussing the profound effect the illness has had on his nine-year-old sister Rachel.

More recently Graeme has received treatment for a condition known as Graft versus Host Disease. This caused him to suffer repeated unpleasant physical experiences mainly in the form of severe abdominal pain. Graeme became depressed and irritable and withdrew from everyday activities. Tests showed his Graft Versus Host Disease was improving and that his discomfort was the result of lactose intolerance. There were two main ways to reduce Graeme's distress. One was to increase his pain control, the other was to reduce his emotional stress by giving him adequate explanations of his experiences so that he was able to make sense of what was going on and begin to anticipate the future without despair. I engaged him in the piece of work overleaf that will be incorporated into his video diary.

The change in his personality whilst producing this work was quite remarkable. Apathy and irritability were quickly replaced with energy, enthusiasm and excitement.

Working with siblings

When children receive their first diagnosis they are confronted with many new experiences. It may be their first hospitalisation, when they are subjected to painful tests and they have to develop trust in the changing hospital staff. They see and sense the anxiety of their families and suddenly their lives are out of their control and they are scared. It is therefore not surprising that as friends, relatives, neighbours and parents, all our concern and attention is focused on the sick child. But what about the siblings?

I amAburp I canbe very rude

Meand my friendsLike to get togeTHer andbuRp. WhenI burp withmyfriends ie causes Graemeto HAVE A Had Tummy pain

Illustration by Graeme

We will have to watch out because the Doctor has done some tests and told Graeme all about us. We Burps live in Graemes bowel and when we burp we give off Hydrogen Gas. Graeme had to blow into a syringe with special liquid to Discover us.
Look out lads if Graeme goes on a Lactose free diet that will be the end of us!

They used to blame our mates Graft and Host but now they've blown our cover we will have to move on and leave Graeme in peace just like Graft and Host did.

Sam Graft   Billy Host
We are smarter than the average bugs.

The healthy siblings of children with a chronic life-threatening illness face many sources of distress. There is the initial turmoil of diagnosis, separation from loved ones during treatment and the absolute chaos and unpredictability leaving them bereft of normal family life. Their parents often lack the energy to identify or respond to the emotional needs of anyone other than the sick child. This can create overwhelming feelings of anger, jealousy, sadness and fear. Intervention with all family members is vital if we are to combat such potentially damaging feelings and create a safe, non-threatening environment in which they can begin to share and explore these thoughts and experiences. In the school setting,

brothers and sisters are having to mix with peers whose lives have a completely different agenda.

Life story books have proved very successful in helping these children understand their worlds and where they fit in relation to the family, the illness, the hospital and medical personnel. Art and imagery often provide an initial form of communication for those children who won't or can't talk about their feelings. These feelings are recorded, verbally unexpressed, but then safely retained in a life story book to be used over and over again once they are ready – verbal communication often follows very quickly and with surprising fluency as some of these examples show.

After producing this drawing, a young teenage girl spoke for the first time of her fear that Jane, her older sister, might die. She had previously been unable to share this with other members of her family but after writing about it in her life story book allowed them all to read it.

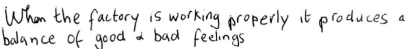
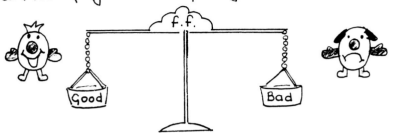

When the factory is working properly it produces a balance of good & bad feelings

This is Nicola's illustration of the Feelings Factory when it is working properly. Nicola had already acknowledged that when the Feelings Factory stops working it produces too many bad feelings leaving not enough room for the good feelings to grow. She then went on to learn new ways of getting rid of the bad feelings, ie by crying the bad feelings come out in your tears, by talking the bad feelings come out in your words, and by writing or drawing the bad feelings are put down on paper where they are less powerful.

Using life story work with families affected by HIV

Jean Lovie

The death of a parent or close family member presents a child with a very particular challenge. With HIV infection death is likely to occur after months, possibly years, of intermittent but progressively serious illness which disrupts family life. There may be more than one family member ill or dying, often cloaked in secrecy thereby increasing the child's loneliness.

Patients ill with HIV infection are frequently profoundly fatigued. They are likely to be younger parents trying to come to terms with their own anger and sadness. They may intend to help a child prepare for change but sometimes these plans can be almost too painful or hard to implement.

Ways of helping children have to be found which are:

– flexible

– pleasurable

– relatively easy to use

– of value to all ages, including children with no or limited reading skills

– adaptable to fast-changing events.

Life story work using family photographs has proved to be one useful method with some families.

Kate and Ben's Story

Kate was four, Ben, her brother, two. Their father had been diagnosed HIV-infected before they were born but their mother, Kate and Ben were non-infected. Kate's playgroup leader, the health visitor and the childminder knew of their father's HIV positive status, as the parents had decided that they would be better able to understand the pressures placed upon the family if they were in the picture. The family was also in regular contact with a hospital social worker.

Four weeks before her father's death, Kate began waking up at night screaming. She knew her father was very ill – time had been taken to answer the questions she had asked. She was unable to say why she was frightened or what exactly was wrong. She wanted to visit her father in hospital and to continue bringing the drawings she had done in playgroup, but she asked to visit less frequently. Her explanation was that the nurses would look after him now. She appeared clearly aware of what was happening but unsure how to express what she thought or was feeling. A way had to be found of helping her to do this.

A known and trusted aunt came to stay. Her mother was able to spend more time at the hospital and Kate was given time and space for herself. On a daily basis, at Kate's pace, family photographs were collected and placed chronologically in a book. Her parents' lives were plotted out, recording an event, the year it happened and, if appropriate, Kate's age at the time. Kate's own photographs were added and those of Ben, her grandparents and close aunts and uncles. The starting point was her parents' birth, then their schooling, hobbies, courtship, marriage, her father's illness, and her own and Ben's birth. To this were added fun experiences they had shared as a family.

As the strength of the family system around her became clearer, Kate chose to say she knew her father was dying. As the work progressed her nightmares receded. Care was taken to answer her questions honestly, including the input of various family members into her life. The book was completed in outline by the time of her father's death. Other close family members brought photographs for the book to the funeral.

Since then Kate's mother has remarried. Her stepfather has learned about her father from the book, and also his photograph has been added. Major family events subsequent to her father's death have been included. Kate still reads the book when she is upset or worried, leaving it out for her mother to see as a signal that she wants help. It has come to be used less as she has adapted to her new life.

The successful outcome in this case depended on:

– the availability of a trusted and close family member who knew everyone in the family and was able to separate out her own feelings and those of Kate about what was happening;

– the availability of an outside facilitator – in this instance a social worker – with whom the interpretation of the ongoing work could be shared;

– the availability of photographs over a period of time;

– an understanding of the family's circumstances. The life story work was part of the help offered to the family in a number of ways. The timing of the life story work in relation to events at the hospital was crucial.

Kate used the photographs to express her awareness of her father's changing appearance in the months before his death as he had become more unwell; she was then able to say she realised he would not return home. Through the photographs the size and strengths of the family network were conveyed.

This approach has been used in similar circumstances with another child of about the same age. In both instances the children were willing to co-operate for a limited time and had, before the work, considerable self-awareness. While life story work may not be appropriate for all families in these circumstances, it has already proved valuable for some.

Life story work with adults
Gerrilyn Smith

Adults, too, can benefit from making a record of their own early lives, or those of their children. This is especially important for those adults who grew up 'in care' themselves. Going back to the places of their childhood can be very therapeutic and help them put their current lives into perspective.

As life story work is relatively new, there will be many adults who grew up 'in care' who will not have had the benefit of someone taking the time to chart with them their lives and moves through the care system. Gaining access to social service files is one way of trying to piece together their past.

The following is an example of some life story work with an adult who was herself 'in care'.

Vanessa's Story
Vanessa was 24 when she was referred to me. She had three children under five years, and had recently had a still birth. She wasn't coping with the children and they were removed from her care while she tried to sort herself out. (This was prior to the Children Act 1989.) Among the list of things we agreed to work on, Vanessa expressed an interest in doing a life story book for herself. This was currently being done with her children and I felt it might help her understand what was happening for them.

We started with a family tree, going back to Vanessa's grandparents. Vanessa knew her paternal grandparents, however, she possessed no information about her maternal grandparents. Vanessa was of mixed parentage – her mother was Spanish and her father from an island in the Caribbean. She began her life story book with the following introduction:

'This diary is to help me and others understand the difficulty of life in being a single parent and having to bring children up on your own. It also tells you about the life I had and why I am the way I am now.'

She began to write of her earliest memories starting with recollections of her life in a convent and of occasional visits from her mother. The first chapter ends at her fifth birthday when she is supposed to return to live with her mother. The second chapter begins with Vanessa's paternal grandmother coming to take her to live with her. Whilst living with her granny, Vanessa had more contact with her father.

Vanessa continued writing another twenty eight chapters of her life. We went over them together talking about her memories, sorting out some confusions and thinking about how her own childhood affected her capacity to parent.

We were able to identify patterns in her life that were being repeated with her children. Vanessa's own mother wouldn't help us with Vanessa's life story book. We wrote to her and went round to visit her, but she refused to participate. Her mother's partner wouldn't let Vanessa speak to her. In reviewing her childhood, Vanessa was able to see that her parents' partners (they were no longer together) frequently stopped Vanessa and her siblings from getting closer to their birth parents. Vanessa was in her third relationship but felt that, unlike her parents' partners, her current partner was able to view Vanessa's children as his own.

We made a list of places she wanted to visit for her life story book. We collected together important mementos she wanted to keep. These included her children's health record books, the important Christmas and birthday cards, photographs of the children from the children's homes they were currently in, and photographs from our round of visits.

We started with a visit to her paternal grandmother's house. We went to several residential units where Vanessa had lived. Many were still being used as homes but not necessarily for young people. In one case the building had been knocked down and only a pile of rubble remained. We visited Vanessa's old secondary school and, with permission, walked around.

It was also important to begin collecting mementos for her children. We went to the hospitals where her children were born, houses and flats where she had previously lived, the nursery the children had attended. Vanessa began to make scrapbooks for her children. She began preparing for them to not move on to foster families, but to return to her and start again.

Whilst the children did spend a period of time away from her she continued to be involved in their care. She visited regularly and predictably. She tried hard to stay connected to her children in a way that her parents had not stayed connected to her. She reflected on her network of friends, many of whom were younger and didn't have the responsibility of looking after children, and who were not encouraging her to keep up contact. She started to meet other young mothers. She began to identify what needed to change before she felt able to resume care of her children. Whilst the life story book was not the only piece of work done with her, it provided a useful focus. It helped her recognise unhelpful patterns in her own childhood – patterns she was determined not to repeat.

Part of what helped Vanessa was someone taking an interest in her childhood. It is very difficult for many parents who experience difficulty in parenting to allow their children to benefit from experiences that they themselves were not offered or were deprived of. By doing Vanessa's life story book, I was able to point out how well she had already done and how she had begun to make changes in the family patterns. Although Vanessa was still very angry with her mother, she had a greater understanding of the difficulties she must have experienced. Vanessa also felt able to reconnect with her father and to ask him for more information about their family.

Unlike other types of individual work with adults, which often occurs in the counsellor's office, Vanessa and I talked in the car on our journeys, in cafes, and in the places that were important to her. The tangible reminders of her past also meant she remembered more and was able to recount in greater detail aspects of her childhood that she had not thought about in a long time. In doing so, we arrived at a better understanding of why Vanessa was the way she was, and began the process of getting her to think about how she would like to be, as a woman, as a partner and as a mother.

Life story work with children adopted from overseas
Tony Ryan and Rodger Walker

Increasing numbers of children who were born in other countries are being adopted in the UK. This process has been going on for long enough for some of the children to have become adolescents, a time when a healthy sense of identity becomes especially important.

In doing life story work with these children there are added considerations for both the children and the adoptive parents. In working with the children you cannot assume some of the basics in the way you can when working with children born and brought up in this country.

Societies are naturally structured differently in different countries and concepts of family, parenthood, and parental obligation can be different and you need to be aware of these and sensitive to them when helping a child to understand his or her origins. This is especially important when looking at reasons why birth parents might have given up their child for adoption.

It is equally important when the parents of the child may not be known at all. Civil unrest, extreme poverty and extended family breakdown can all have meant that a child's origins are unknown and cannot be part of his or her life story work – the trail may only start from when the adopters met the child for the first time.

However, it is essential to get as much information as possible about the child's country and customs and language and for these to be part of the work. If individual information and material are not available then pictures of children in the country of origin will need to be substituted.

The issues raised in Chapter 10, *Working with Black Children*, are equally relevant in work with children from other countries, even when the children are not black.

Many countries of origin are portrayed in the media in a derogatory way and those doing life story work with the child may need to come to terms with this as the child will need to feel positive about his or her native country and will pick up from you how you feel about their country. Most adoptive parents almost certainly will not share the child's origins and will need to appreciate the effect this might have – the child will not feel you understand his or her feelings about growing up in the UK when their origins are elsewhere.

Similarly, children in the neighbourhood and at school may want to know where the child comes from – you can help by making the child secure about his or her origins and able to acknowledge that he or she comes from a different country and to be proud of this heritage, not embarrassed about it. If this is not possible then a good cover story will help.

Using maps (see page 29) will help the children orientate themselves. Remember to show maps of the countries in between their country and the UK, or to use a world map, as well as maps of the country of origin and this country, so that the child can see how they came to Britain.

Posters and pictures of the country of origin can be obtained from embassies and if you are close enough they may be willing to refer you to someone to talk to you and the child. This would be invaluable in helping you both to understand the culture, customs and everyday life of the country your child has come from.

If you decide to and are able to visit the country of the child's origin this will need careful preparation but would be invaluable in helping the child to develop a healthy sense of identity.

Consider carefully the question of contact with the birth family – you will need to judge if the child is ready to handle it.

Some countries make such trips difficult because they close the door behind the child after adoption. Records may be unreliable or may not have been kept, or they may have been destroyed. Some countries may have allowed dual citizenship but this brings obligations, such as military service, which they may expect to be fulfilled.

Record the trip and take photographs of all the people and places important to the child's origins and the story, particularly the place they were born and the place where they first met the adopters.

Some people suggest that if you are making a life story book you should make two – one about the child's story and one about the child's country of origin. If you do this, consider whether it conveys to the child a feeling of separation from his or her roots; each child will be different.

Adopters

You may be an adoptive parent doing life story work with your child.

The reasons for adopting your child will need to be part of the work. As well as the usual issues about why you decided to adopt you will also need to address the fact that you chose to adopt a child from overseas.

You may have done this because there are so few babies for adoption in the UK now, or you may have heard stories of abandoned children in the media or you may have worked in the country of origin and became close to that child. You may have wanted to provide a child with disabilities a chance of a successful life and treatment which they could not have had if you had not adopted them.

Be aware of the implications of "rescuing" a child from their birth country or of people from a rich country adopting children from a poor country. Your child will identify with his or her country and with its people and if they feel bad about the country it will not help their sense of self-worth.

Through life story work you can help your child
develop a healthy sense of identity and integrate their
cultural and personal history into their whole
personality.

Further Reading

Adoption & Fostering, BAAF's quarterly journal, contains several useful articles on life story work and related issues. An index is published annually.

Ahmed Shama, Cheetham Juliette, and Small John (eds), *Social Work with Black Children and their Families*, BAAF/Batsford, 1986.

Barn Ravinder, *Black Children in the Public Care System*, BAAF/Batsford, 1993.

Carroll Jo, 'Piecing it together', *Community Care*, 24 January 1991. This article refers to another article 'Reality Orientation and Reminiscence Therapy' in the British Journal of Psychiatry, 1987.

Cipolla J, Benson McGown D, Yanulis M A, *Communicating through Play*, BAAF, 1992.

Fahlberg Vera, *Fitting the Pieces Together*, BAAF, 1988.

Inter-country Adoption (Notes) Leicester University.

Jewett Claudia, *Helping Children Cope with Separation and Loss*, BAAF/Batsford, 1984.

Jewett Claudia, *Adopting the Older Child*, Harvard Common Press, 1978, USA.

Life Books for Children in Care, Northern Ireland Foster Care Association, 1984.

Morrison J, Working with Sexual Trauma: some principles of individual therapy with adolescent and pre-adolescent victims of child sexual abuse, *Practice*, pp 311–325, 1988.

National Foster Care Association, *The Challenge of Foster Care*, NFCA, 1988 (Due to be revised by 1994)

National Foster Care Association, *My Book about Me*, NFCA, 1990.

Oaklander Violet, *Windows to our Children: a Gestalt therapy approach to children and adults*, Real People Press, 1978, USA.

Sagar Carol, 'Working with cases of child sexual abuse', in Case C and Dalley T (eds), *Working with Children in Art Therapy*, Tavistock/Routledge, 1990.

Sgroi S, 'Treatment of the Sexually Abused Children' in *Handbook of Clinical Intervention in Child Sexual Abuse*, Lexington, 1982.

Showers Paul, *Your Skin and Mine*, A and C Black, 1967.

Smith G, 'The Unbearable Traumatic Past' Varma V (ed), *The Secret Lives of Vulnerable Children*, Routledge, 1991.

Talking about Adoption to your Adopted Child Prue Chennells and Marjorie Morrison, BAAF, 1998.

The Children Act 1989: importance of culture, race, religion and language, *Practice Note 26*, BAAF.

The Placement Needs of Black Children, *Practice Note 13*, BAAF.

Troyna Barry, and Hatches R, *Racism in Children's Lives: A study of mainly white primary schools*, Routledge/National Children's Bureau, 1992.

Wilson A N, *The Development of Psychology of the Black Child*, African Research Publication, 1980.

Working with Sexually Abused Children: a resource pack for professionals, The Children's Society, 1989.